C000059562

AN ORNAMENT
TO THE CITY

HOLY TRINITY CHURCH &
THE CAPUCHIN ORDER

Patricia Curtin-Kelly

The
History
Press
Ireland

Patricia Curtin-Kelly is a Cork-born art historian who lives in Dublin with her husband and daughter. She holds an MA (hons) in Art History from University College Dublin as well as an MSc in Human Resources Management from Sheffield Hallam University.

First published 2015

The History Press Ireland
50 City Quay
Dublin 2
Ireland
www.thehistorypress.ie

British Library Cataloguing in Publication Data.
A catalogue record for this book is available from the British Library.

ISBN 978 1 84588 861 9

Typesetting and origination by The History Press

Central front cover image © Adrian Muttitt/Alamy.
Left and right front cover images © Clodagh Evelyn Kelly.
Back cover image courtesy library of Congress;
Irish Capuchin Provincial Archives, Dublin.

Contents

Foreword

It is with great joy that we Capuchins greet the publication of Patricia Curtin-Kelly's monograph on Holy Trinity church. To this day its neo-Gothic façade is a landmark for all those who visit the city of Cork. It is also a reminder of the Christian heritage of the city and of the countless Capuchin Friars who, over the years, have laboured in the church for the good of the people.

Like the building itself our work has often suffered setbacks, has had to respond to unexpected challenges and has even, at times, had to radically change in order to better respond to the needs of the people we serve. The vision of our founder, St Francis of Assisi, informed the work of the first Capuchins who came to Ireland in the seventeenth century, at a time of terrible crisis for the Irish people. This vision also informed Fr Theobald Mathew, the founder of Holy Trinity church, and the many friars and others who came after him, who contributed to the building of the church.

I am privileged to have been invited by Patricia Curtin-Kelly to contribute this foreword as an invitation to all who come to read this work to recognise the context of the larger story in which the building of Holy Trinity church fits and the thread of Capuchin Franciscan continuity that passes through its foundation, building, remodelling and restoration. It is a church that continues to be both an 'ornament to the city of Cork' and the home of a living worshipping Christian community to this day.

On behalf of the Irish Capuchin province I take this opportunity to congratulate Patricia Curtin-Kelly on the publication of this work. I would like to extend an invitation to readers to come and visit Holy Trinity church in the future, to see its many beautiful features which are described so well. The publication of this book coincides with the quad-centenary of the arrival of the first Capuchins to Ireland in 1615. It is timely, therefore, that we will be celebrating this 400-year-old anniversary in 2015 and the publication of this book at the same time.

Br Adrian Curran OFM Capuchin
Provincial Minister
December 2014

Acknowledgements

This book is partially based on a thesis, for a Masters in Art History, completed at University College Dublin in 2013. In that context, I wish to thank my supervisor, Prof. Kathleen James-Chakraboarty and the staff in the different libraries and archives for their assistance and courtesy. A particular word of thanks to Dr Brian Kirby, Archivist at the Irish Capuchin Provincial Archives in Dublin, for his helpfulness and support and to Ken Ryan, of Abbey Stained Glass in Dublin, who showed me the intricacies of stained-glass production. A special word of thanks to my cousin Jim (Fr Edwin Flynn OFM Cap.) for his interest and encouragement. Thanks are also due to the staff at The History Press Ireland, in particular Ronan Colgan and Beth Amphlett. Finally, thank you to my husband, Bryan Kelly, for his unfailing support over the years as well as my daughter Clodagh Kelly who also contributed her photographic skills.

NOTE: Up until the first/second decade of the twentieth century members of the Capuchin Order carried the abbreviated letters OSFC (Ordinis Santi Francisci Capuccinorum) after their name. This subsequently changed to OFM Cap. (Order of Friars Minor Capuchin) which is still in use today to denote membership of the Capuchin Order. This change is reflected in the text of the book.

Introduction

In the early 1800s, before Catholic Emancipation was established in Ireland, a priest who worked in the back lanes of Cork City had a dream. He wanted to build a church that would raise people's hearts above the grinding poverty that surrounded them and make them feel the joy of belonging to a Church that was renewing itself after ages of oppression.[1]

This priest was Fr Theobald Mathew OSFC (1790-1856), a member of the Capuchin Order, who was also known as the 'Apostle of Temperance'. Fr Mathew, the patron of Holy Trinity church, was a man born into wealth and privilege, but he spent his life working to improve the lives of poverty-stricken people.

The planning for Holy Trinity church began in 1825, but it was not completed until 1890. The sixty-five-year journey, in bringing this evolving building to completion, mirrors the turbulent history of the Ireland of the time. Its foundation stone was laid in 1832, but due to financial and other problems, the church opened for services in 1850 in an incomplete state. Finally, after many efforts, the portico and spire were added in 1890, the centenary year of the birth of its patron.

The building and completion of Holy Trinity church is also steeped in the history of Cork City and the Order of Friars Minor Capuchins in Ireland. The story begins with the foundation of the city, followed by its capture by various foreign forces, the coming of the Capuchin Order to Ireland from France during Penal times, to Catholic Emancipation, to the First World War, and to the struggle for an independent Irish republic.

Major renovations and more modern influences, such as the Second Vatican Council, have had an impact on the church's interior. Fr Mathew did not live to see his church completed but, as a testament to his memory, the cause was taken up and subsequently expanded by his successors, including the building of a large adjoining friary.

The original architect for the building was George R. Pain (1793-1838), who in 1825 won the competition to design Holy Trinity church. While Pain's original plan has been modified somewhat, the church still has his stamp. It is a fine example of English Gothic and shows the influence of the Gothic Revival on his design. It is also probably one of the first churches in Ireland to use cast-iron in its construction.

This church, which has evolved over decades, manages to combine its disparate elements into a unique and striking building. One would never suspect that the work of several architects was involved in the undertaking or that it took so long to complete. The church was facing possible demolition in the 1980s due to major structural deterioration. Luckily, this did not happen and it was refurbished and restored instead.

The interior of the church was drastically altered during renovation work in the 1980s, but it still retains some very interesting stained-glass windows. Three of these are of particular Irish interest. Original drawings have been discovered for two Harry Clarke Studio windows, as well as correspondence which provides authentication for a third Harry Clarke-designed window. These three windows are not featured in the *Gazeteer of Irish Stained Glass* and, for reasons that are outlined, should be included.

This is the only church dedicated to the memory of Fr Mathew, who was an unusual man for his time and a true social reformer. The contribution to cultural and civil life by other notable Capuchins in Cork is also outlined, including those who were involved in the 1916 Rising and the War of Independence.

Unfortunately, most of the records relating to the Cork friary have been lost over the years. Fortunately, some scrapbooks survive, which are housed in the Irish Capuchin Provincial Archives in Dublin, and much of the research for this book has been sourced from these records.

1

Cork City – Historical Background

Cork, the second largest city in the Republic of Ireland, has an ancient and turbulent history. The city's ecclesiastical foundation dates back to 606 when St Finbarr built his settlement there. This was built on the site of the present Church of Ireland cathedral, which is named after him. Later, a walled city was built on an island formed by the north and south channels of the River Lee. The Danes captured Cork in about 820. Following the arrival of the Anglo-Normans in 1172, it received its first charter in 1177 from Henry II (1133-89).

The Anglo-Normans brought not only their civil government and laws but also the Mendicant Friars of the Franciscans and Dominicans. The *Pecata Hibernia* map,[2] *c.* 1600 (Fig. 1), shows the walled city of Cork and the probable origin of its coat of arms. This depicts a ship sailing between two towers. The towers are the King's and Queen's Castles, which were at either side of the Water Gate and the city's motto is *Statio bene fide carinis* (A safe harbour for ships). In 1900, the city received its last charter from Queen Victoria (1819-1901).

In 1601, around the time of the Battle of Kinsale, the Penal Laws began to be enforced in Ireland. These were a series of laws forced on Irish Catholics and Protestant Dissenters to compel

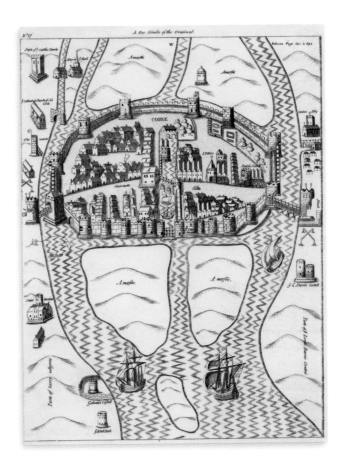

Fig. 1. Pecata
Hibernia map, *c.*
1601. (Cork City
Libraries)

them to accept the reformed Christian faith. The Insurrection of
1641 was an attempt to seize control of English administration in
Ireland, sparked by Catholic fears of an invasion by anti-Catholic
forces from England. This was followed by the Cromwellian
Plantation (1649-53) which was a particularly brutal time for Irish
Catholics. Many old Cork families struggled for their religious lib-
erty and defended their faith. By 1704, there were only four priests
in the city.[3] Catholics at this time could be neither members of
Parliament nor vote for members of Parliament, they could not
take out leases, and were forbidden to improve their lands during
this period. If they bought land, or indeed a horse, worth more
than £5 any Protestant could seize it. No education was available

for their children nor could they legally send them abroad to be educated. Under the Penal Laws of 1668, all Catholics were not only ordered out of Cork City, but also forbidden to become articled to trades or professions. As a result, trade in the city declined. Dean Jonathan Swift (1667-1745), the well-known Anglo-Irish satirist and author who was also Dean of St Patrick's Cathedral in Dublin (1713-45), described their plight as 'the wretched merchants have become mere peddlers'. [4]

In 1690, the surrender of the city to John Churchill, 1st Duke of Marlborough (1656-1722), saw the gradual disappearance of the city walls and its expansion north and south of the river. From the 1770s onwards, the city began to expand eastwards. William Beaufort's *Map of Cork City 1801* (Fig. 2) shows this expansion as well as the river channel, which ran along the course of St Patrick's Street, completely covered over. The covering of St Patrick's Street took place between 1774 and 1789.

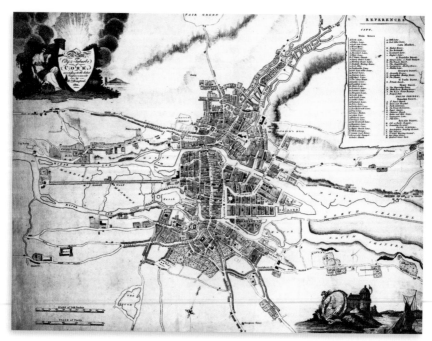

Fig. 2. Beaufort map of Cork City, 1801. (Cork City Libraries)

An easing of the bitterness of centuries between Catholics and Protestants is also evident from this time. It would not be until the end of the eighteenth century, however, before any real relaxation of the Penal Laws was evident.[5] The Act of Union in 1800 abolished a separate Irish Parliament in Dublin and from then until 1922 Ireland was governed directly from Westminster.

Due to the late eighteenth-century conflict between Britain and France, there was a huge increase in the export trade of food produce from Cork. The end of the Napoleonic Wars in 1815, however, caused a general recession in the city.[6] The collapse of prices in 1815 was followed by a famine during 1816-17. People flocked into the city from the surrounding countryside in search of food and work. This in turn led to a housing crisis and epidemics, such as typhoid, sweeping the city. Economically, and to a certain extent socially, the decades between the Act of Union and the Great Famine represented a period of harshness and uncertainty for impoverished Irish people. It was a time when even 'God seemed to abandon Ireland'.[7] As a result, several thousand people emigrated from Cork in the first two decades of the 1800s.

In 1822, the British economy began to recover and funding was made available to assist the Irish. The Wide Streets Commission was reinstated to redevelop the older areas of Cork City. Large slum areas were demolished and new streets and bridges erected. From the 1830s onwards, several of the city's landmarks were built, including hospitals, churches and commercial buildings.[8]

By 1900, Cork was readily recognised by today's standards, as its streets, river channels, most of its bridges, and virtually all of the city centre churches and other public buildings were in place.[9] It also had a tram system and five main railway stations. It is into this turbulent and difficult background that we must consider the presence of the Capuchin Order in Ireland and in Cork.

2

The Capuchin Order
in Ireland

The Order of Friars Minor Capuchin traces its origins back to a Franciscan reform movement which was initiated in 1528 by the Italian Observant Franciscan, Br Matteo Serafini (Matteo da Bascio) (1495-1552) (Fig. 3). He sought a return to the original way of life of the Order of Friars Minor, founded by St Francis of Assisi in 1209. Like many other followers of previous Franciscan reform movements, such as the Spirituals, the Amadeists, the Colletines and the Observantines, friars inspired by Friar Matteo's example also adopted a life of strict poverty. Members of the Capuchin Order were distinguished by wearing untrimmed beards and a brown habit with a pointed hood, or *cappuccio*, which they believed was the primitive Franciscan habit. What started as a humorous nickname probably accounts for the origin of the name of Capuchin. While the wearing of a beard is no longer mandatory, the Capuchin Friars still wear the distinctive brown habit today.

In 1528, Pope Clement VII (1478-1534) gave the Capuchins approval to set up a separate order. In 1619, he raised the Capuchin Vicar to the status of Minister General. The Capuchins, freed from their dependence on the Conventual Franciscans, became an

Fig. 3.
A seventeenth-century
engraving of
Br Matteo Serafini
(Matteo de Bascio)
(1495-1552), founder
of the Order of Friars
Minor Capuchin,
by Michael Van
Lochom (1601-47).
(Irish Capuchin
Provincial Archives,
Dublin)

autonomous branch of the Fransiscan family.[10] In spite of setbacks, by the end of the sixteenth century, the Capuchin Order had spread all over the Catholic parts of Europe. The antiquarian and historian John Windele said that the Capuchins did not arrive in Ireland until after the Reformation in 1623, and came to Cork in 1760.[11] Other records, however, show differently, as outlined below.

The founder of the Capuchin Order in Ireland was Francis Lavalin Nugent OSFC (1569-1633). He was born in Walshestown, County Westmeath and was sent to France for an education that was not possible in Ireland due to the Penal Laws. In 1589, Fr Nugent (Fig. 4) joined the Capuchin Order in what is now Belgium and, in about 1594, was sent to the Friary at Charleville in the Champagne district of France. In 1608, Pope Paul V (1599-1658) nominated him Vicar Apostolic and Commissary General, with full power to establish the order in Ireland.[12] The friary was subsequently transferred from Charleville to Bar-sur-Aude, from 1686 until 1790 (Fig. 5).

In 1615, Br Stephen Daly OSFC became the first Irish Capuchin to return to his native land and was followed by four other friars. In 1624, the first Capuchin Community was founded in Dublin's Bridge Street by Fr Nugent. In 1637, the Capuchins had established themselves in Cork and, by 1642, there were fifty-one friars with houses in six towns and cities throughout the country.

In 1649, Oliver Cromwell (1599-1655) arrived in Ireland and under his regime a new wave of persecution ensued in which

Fig. 4.
An engraving of
Fr Francis Lavalin
Nugent OSFC
(1569-1635), founder
of the Capuchin
Order in Ireland. (Irish
Capuchin Provincial
Archives, Dublin)

Fr. Franciscus Nugent Hibernus Provinc. Belgii def. ac Vic. Ap., Zelo Religionis et Ordinis celebris, qui abdicata Sede Armacan. ipsi oblata, supremum diem explebat Anno 1635.

Fig. 5. The exterior of the former Irish Capuchin Friary, Bar-sur-Aube,
France, *c.* 1916. (Irish Capuchin Provincial Archives, Dublin)

the religious orders, especially mendicant friars, were targeted. In spite of persecution, the Order continued to grow and by 1733 the Capuchins had fourteen houses in Ireland.[13] Under the Penal Laws, priests were not allowed to wear religious dress in public and the Capuchins, who worked among the population disguised in ordinary civilian clothes, developed a reputation for closeness to the people.[14] For a while the Irish friars were united with those in Britain. However, in 1873 they regained 'custody' status and were reconstituted as the 'Province of St. Patrick' in 1885.[15]

The first Capuchin friary in Cork was established in 1637 but, like many other religious houses in Ireland, it was destroyed during the wars of the seventeenth century. Later a Cork Capuchin, Fr Bartholomew Mortell OSFC who was educated on the Continent, opened a hospice in the city. It was probably on

Fig. 6. Fr Arthur O'Leary OSFC (1729-1802), founder of the Capuchin's South Friary, Blackamoor Lane, Cork (engraving by W. Bond, from a print, after a drawing by Murphy). (Irish Capuchin Provincial Archives, Dublin)

Fig. 7. The exterior of the old Capuchin friary church, Blackamoor Lane, Cork.
(Irish Capuchin Provincial Archives, Dublin)

this site that Fr Robert Comyn OSFC and Fr Michael O'Cuileain OSFC acquired a house that they converted into a chapel and the remaining rooms were used as cells for themselves and their brethren.[16] Fr Comyn was a brother of Sir Dominic Coppinger, an important citizen and recorder of Cork.[17] No doubt such family connections helped to establish the Order in the city.

When Murrough O'Brien, the First Earl of Inchiquin (1614-74), came to Cork in 1644, he expelled the entire Catholic population and the Capuchin friars were forced to flee. They hid in the countryside, slipped into the city whenever possible, and eventually re-opened their friary in 1649.[18] It was probably constructed on the same site that the subsequent 'South Friary' at Blackamoor Lane was built by Fr Arthur O'Leary OSFC (1729-1802).[19]

Fr O'Leary (Fig. 6), from Faulobbus, Dunmanway, County Cork, was ordained a Capuchin priest in St Malo in Brittany. He remained in France for several years and served there as chaplain to the many British and Irish prisoners held captive in France during the war with Britain (1756-62).

Fr O'Leary was a renowned preacher and controversialist who worked for peace and religious tolerance all his life. He was a precursor to Daniel O'Connell (1775-1847) in relation to Catholic Emancipation, and worked tirelessly for the repeal of the Penal Laws. However, he did not live long enough to see that dream realised. Fr O'Leary described the church at Blackamoor Lane (Fig. 7) as being 'remarkable for its dwarfish dimensions, its utter want of architectural grace, and its perfect seclusion from the public gaze'. He went on to say that 'It was not much bigger than a respectable barn and, but for its galleries, might have passed for one'.[20] Clearly a new church was required to meet the growing demand, from an ever-increasing congregation, and the person to recognise and act on this need was Fr Theobald Mathew OSFC.

3

Fr Theobald Mathew

Born on 10 October 1790, Theobald Mathew was reared in Thomastown Castle, County Tipperary. At the time, Ireland was dominated by the Anglo-Irish Ascendency. These were descendants of British colonists who had settled in the country in the wake of the conquest by England and the subsequent plantation of Ireland. Theobald's father, James, was agent for the Irish estates of his cousin Francis Mathew, known after 1747 as the Earl of Llanduff. To maintain their property, which included over 2,000 acres of good land, Llanduff converted to the Church of Ireland during the Penal Times. All of his descendants in Ireland followed suit. However, the family continued to marry Catholics and supported Catholic relief.[21]

The Mathews were of Welsh origin and belonged to a branch of the family that had remained Catholic. James Mathew, who was a Catholic, was adopted by his cousin Francis, a Protestant. Theobald grew up, therefore, in the relatively lavish surroundings of Thomastown Castle, in the company of his Protestant cousins. He was a favourite of Lady Elizabeth, daughter of the Earl of Llanduff, who paid for his education.[22] The village of Cappaghwhite, in County Tipperary, gets its name from the family of his mother, Anne Mathew (*née* Whyte).

Theobald, who was known as Toby by his family, was the fourth son in a family of nine boys and three girls.[23] From his infancy, he was his mother's favourite child. Anne Mathew was a pious Catholic and, like many mothers in Ireland at the time, she hoped to see one of her many sons become a priest.[24] Always engaging and anxious to please his parents and elders, Theobald decided to fulfil his mother's wishes. He attended St Canice's Academy in Kilkenny (1800-7) and matriculated in the humanity class of the National Seminary of Maynooth where he had been studying to become a secular priest. The seminary had a strong Catholic religious orientation with strict rules and regulations. However, Theobald broke the rules of the seminary by having a party in his room for his fellow seminarians. For him, this would have been a normal feature of his family life, which was renowned for its hospitality. Fearing expulsion, he returned home to contemplate his next move.[25]

While in Kilkenny, Theobald had been influenced by the life of self-sacrifice of two aged Capuchin friars, whom he had met during his school days. As a result, he decided to join the Capuchin Novitiate in Church Street in Dublin (1808-13). He was ordained a priest on 17 April 1813.[26]

At the time Theobald Mathew became a priest, the Catholic Church in Ireland was only slowly emerging from a persecution which had lasted, with greater or lesser severity, from the time of the Reformation. However, persecution had fallen more heavily on the religious orders.[27] In addition, while acknowledging the value of religious orders such as the Capuchins, the Irish bishops did not encourage them. This was because the already overburdened people would have had to support them, in addition to their ordinary secular priests.

Photographs show that Theobald Mathew had a striking personal appearance (Fig. 8). He was always keen to share whatever he possessed with others and carried this trait throughout his life.

Fr Dan Donovan OSFC was the priest who received Fr Mathew in Blackamoor Lane when he came to Cork. Fr Donovan had escaped the guillotine during the French Revolution due to his Irish identity. This was thanks to an Irish officer in the French Army who used his influence with the authorities to save Fr Donovan and six other Irishmen.[28] Fr Mathew settled in Cork, from 1814 to 1838, and threw himself into the life and work of the poor of the area. This included learning Irish, so as to be able to communicate better with the local people. This work was in stark contrast to the life of splendour and refinement he would have led had he remained at home in Thomastown Castle and not entered a religious order. He continued with these charitable works until the great crusade of his life, the temperance movement, caused him to take on a different role. Fr Matthew also held the important post of Provincial of the Irish Capuchins for many years.

Fig. 8.
Fr Theobald
Mathew OSFC,
'the Apostle of
Temperance',
(1790-1856), patron
of Holy Trinity
church, Cork,
by Matthew Brady,
1849. (Library of
Congress; Irish
Capuchin Provincial
Archives, Dublin)

In the nineteenth century, Cork was a densely populated city. It was also full of problems, resulting from a lack of work and poverty, as well as oppression due to a brutal foreign occupation landlord system. As well as his religious duties, Fr Mathew was constantly engaged in projects for the amelioration of the poor in the city. He established a school that contributed greatly to the education of boys and girls who would not otherwise have had such an opportunity.[29] He established a graveyard for Catholics as, up until then, all were in the hands of Protestant clergy and the burial fees were enormous. In addition, in order to read the burial service over their own people, priests were compelled by law to request the permission of the local Protestant clergy. The Burial Act was passed in 1825 and, following that, there had been a disposition to refuse this permission or at least to grant it in such an ungracious manner as to make the Catholic clergy feel their inferior position in the eyes of the law. In January 1830, Fr Mathew purchased the former Botanical Gardens in Cork, and opened the graveyard which he dedicated to St Joseph. This was a major contribution to helping the less well off at a time of great sorrow and loss.

What set the seal to Fr Mathew's reputation as a genuine philanthropist and social worker, however, was the devotion he showed towards the people of Cork during the terrible outbreak of cholera in 1832. He opened one of the largest temporary hospitals in the city, near Blackamoor Lane, where he tended to the sick and dying.[30] A cross, used by Fr Mathew at this time, during his calls to cholera victims, is extant in the Irish Capuchin Provincial Archives in Dublin (Fig. 9).

His great crusade, which gave him the name of the 'Apostle of Temperance,' began in response to the prevalence of alcohol in Irish culture. Perhaps this was due, in part, to the heritage left over from the time of persecution of the Catholic population in general. Deprived by law of the safeguards of religion, many people turned from the hardships of their daily lives to seek relief, or even

some forgetfulness, in drink. As a result, distilling was among the
very few Irish industries to prosper throughout the eighteenth and
nineteenth centuries. Inspiration came from the United States of
America, where temperance societies had been in existence since
the last decade of the eighteenth century.[31]

In the 1830s, a Quaker called William Martin set up a temperance society in Cook Street in Cork that was greeted with a
riot. He realised that he needed the association of an influential
priest if the total abstinence movement was to make any headway
in a city as Catholic as Cork. Fr Mathew, without doubt, fitted
this description. As many of his family members were involved in
the business of making alcohol, Fr Mathew no doubt had pause

Fig. 9.
The cross used by Fr Theobald
Mathew OSFC during his
visits to cholera victims in Cork
in 1831/2. (Irish Capuchin
Provincial Archives, Dublin)

for thought. One of his brothers had a large distillery at Castlelake, County Tipperary, in which another two of his brothers were also shareholders. His sister was married to another extensive distiller called Hackett, of Midleton, County Cork. His brother Charles was married to a Hackett, of the same Midleton family.[32] While he originally demurred, in 1838 Fr Mathew eventually took up the challenge when he formed the total abstinence movement in Cork. At the time, he is reputed to have said, 'here goes in the name of God'. In spite of the effect the temperance movement would have had on his family fortunes, Fr Mathew showed great determination in persevering with his crusade, and many breweries and distilleries closed as a result of his efforts. Remarkably, this did not interfere with the closeness between him and his family members as they continued to support Fr Mathew throughout his endeavours.

His inspiring presence and tireless energy led to the spread of the temperance movement far and wide.[33] Fr Mathew defrayed the costs of the temperance movement from his own pocket. He supported many poor people and families and gave away 60,000 temperance medals and cards free of charge (Fig. 10).[34] The detail on Daly's Temperance Card graphically illustrates the linkages between 'strong whiskey' and the 'fruits of intemperance'. In furtherance of his crusade, Fr Mathew travelled throughout Ireland and abroad and, by January 1839, 200,000 people had signed a pledge not to consume alcohol. He went to Limerick in December 1839 and in four days 150,000 had joined. He went to Waterford soon after and in three days 80,000 more joined. In January 1840, he went to Dublin and it is estimated that the numbers taking the pledge by then had exceeded 2 million people.[35]

In 1849, it was reported that 50,000 people turned up at one of his meetings in the East End of London and that thousands had taken the pledge.[36] In the summer of 1849, Fr Mathew went to the United States of America and spent nearly two years there. He again attracted

Fig. 10. Total Abstinence Society Medal & Temperance Card belonging to
P.P. Daly. The rim of this gold medal is engraved 'P.P. Daly took the pledge
on May 20th 1840'. (Irish Capuchin Provincial Archives, Dublin)

enormous crowds and added 600,000 to the number of pledge takers.
A formal reception was held for him in the Senate and he was enter-
tained at the White House by President Zachary Tailor (1784-1850),[37]
the nineteenth President of the United States (1849-50). During the
great excitement of the temperance movement, Fr Mathew was
encouraged by many, from all over Ireland, to allow Holy Trinity
church in Cork to be finished by the subscriptions he had received
from teetotallers but 'he would not allow this to be accomplished'.[38]
He clearly wished to keep his activities in the temperance movement
separate to the church building project in Cork.

At its height, just before the Great Famine, Fr Mathew's crusade
had enrolled nearly 3 million people, half the adult population
of Ireland. At the time he was widely acclaimed as a national sav-
iour. Daniel O'Connell (1775-1847) is reputed to have said that

Fr Mathew was 'the greatest man that Ireland ever produced'.
O'Connell (Fig. 11), the foremost Irish politician in the first half
of the nineteenth century, campaigned for Catholic Emancipation
and the repeal of the Act of Union which united Great Britain and
Ireland. The *Freeman's Journal* reported that on Easter Monday
1842, O'Connell and Thomas Lyons (1782-1850), the Lord Mayor
of Cork (1841-2) walked with Fr Mathew at the head of the annual
temperance parade in Cork. The Cork-born architect, sculptor and
cartoonist Denis Santry (1879-1960) depicted O'Connell, wearing his robe of office as Lord Mayor of Dublin, kneeling to receive
a blessing from Fr Mathew, having separated from the parade

Fig. 11.
Print of Daniel
O'Connell,
'The Liberator',
(1776-1847),
attributed to
Wild and the
lithographers Rigo
Bros & Co., Paris.
(Irish Capuchin
Provincial Archives,
Dublin)

(Fig. 12). However, Fr Mathew was reluctant to align the temperance movement with politics. His views were out of step with the majority of ordinary citizens and Irish clergy who strongly supported O'Connell, who was known as 'The Liberator'. O'Connell and Fr Mathew were two iconic figures who ran parallel campaigns in the mid-nineteenth century – O'Connell was a political reformer and Fr Mathew was a social reformer. Between the two of them, they had an extraordinary effect on the lives of downtrodden Irish people. Had both campaigns been aligned, who knows how the course of Irish history might have been changed.

In December 1851, Fr Mathew returned to Cork from the United States of America, but he was in poor health at this stage. He suffered a stroke in 1852 that severely curtailed his activities. In 1854, he went to Madeira for health reasons and soon after his return home he went to Cobh (known then as Queenstown) to help his recovery.[39] He stayed in a house on the sea front belonging to his friend John Sullivan. He died there on 8 December 1856, when 'the heart of Ireland was touched with sorrow'.[40] He was given a public funeral and the cortège was said to be 3 miles in length. Around 50,000 mourners gathered at the gates of St Joseph's Cemetery, where he had asked to be buried.[41]

Probably due to deterioration, the railings that surrounded his grave have been removed. The inscription on the flat gravestone laid on the ground reads, 'Father Mathew, The Apostle of Temperance, Born 10th October 1790, Died 8th December 1856. May he rest in peace. Amen'. There is also a large stone cross on the same site with the inscription 'Erected A.D. 1830 – the Very Rev. Theobald Mathew', commemorating the purchase and opening of St Joseph's Cemetery by Fr Mathew (Fig. 13).

Fr Mathew has been commemorated by monuments, statues and pictures and in names of streets, bridges, halls and schools. The *London Illustrated News*[42] reported that a foundation stone for

Fig. 12. Daniel O'Connell receiving a blessing from Fr Theobald Mathew OSFC
at a temperance parade in Cork in 1842, by Denis Santry (1879-1960).
(Irish Capuchin Provincial Archives, Dublin)

a 'beautiful Gothic tower, known as the Temperance Tower, was laid to commemorate the work of Fr Mathew's temperance crusade'. The inscribed silver trowel used for the occasion commemorated 'the enthusiastic reception given to the Very Rev. Theobald Mathew by the citizens of London, without distinction of religion or politics'. The tower is still standing at Mount Oval in Glounthaune, just outside Cork City, although it is now part of a private home. The site is near the former residence of William Murphy who donated the land for the tower. Today the Temperance Tower is still a local landmark, high up on the hill, at the Dunkettle roundabout.

The Irish sculptor John Henry Foley (1818-74) was commissioned to design a statue to commemorate Fr Mathew. He also made, among other works, the statue to commemorate

Fig. 13. Cross commemorating the opening of St Joseph's Cemetery and Fr Theobald Mathew's Grave, Cork. (Clodagh Evelyn Kelly, Dublin)

Fig. 14. Statue of Father Mathew OSFC, St Patrick's Street, Cork. The statue,
by John Foley (1818-74), was unveiled on 10 October 1864. This image, taken
around 1890, is also interesting as it shows St Patrick's Street before it was burned
down in the early 1920s by British forces. Today the statue stands on several
steps and the railings have now been removed. In addition, the buildings in the
background, particularly those on the left-hand side, are significantly different
following the rebuilding of Cork. (Irish Capuchin Provincial Archives, Dublin)

Daniel O'Connell on O'Connell Street, Dublin and the monument to Prince Albert in Kensington, London. Fr Mathew's
statue was originally commissioned from another Irish sculptor, John Hogan (1800-56), but unfortunately he died before he
could take on the job. Foley's sculpture is situated in the main
street (St Patrick's Street) of Cork and is known colloquially as
'the statue'. It is interesting to note that the figure of Fr Mathew
is depicted wearing civilian rather than clerical dress, as the
wearing of the latter was forbidden during his lifetime. It has the
inscription 'A tribute from a grateful people' on its plinth (Fig. 14).
On 10 October 1864, it was unveiled by the Lord Mayor of Cork,
John Francis Maguire MP (1815-72),[43] in the presence of over
100,000 people, representing every county in Ireland.[44]

There is a fine bust of Fr Mathew in the Irish Capuchin Provincial Archives in Dublin by Hogan which was located in the Fr Mathew Hall in Dublin for many years (Fig. 15). There is also a statue dedicated to the memory of Fr Mathew in the middle of O'Connell Street in Dublin. Unveiled in 1893, it was created by the Irish sculptor Mary Redmond (1863-1930). Interestingly, Fr Mathew is depicted by Redmond wearing the traditional long habit of the Capuchin Order, which would not have been allowed in his day.

Fr Mathew has also been commemorated in poetry, such as the Irish poem '*Duain Chuimhne An Athar Toboid Maitiu*' by Tadgh O'Donnachadha, and in song, such as 'The Ballad of Fr Mathew' by Cliff Wedgebury. In addition, several busts and paintings were commissioned. An example of a painting is 'Fr Mathew Receives a

Fig. 15.
Bust of Fr Theobald Mathew OSFC by John Hogan (1800-50). (Irish Capuchin Provincial Archives, Dublin)

Fig. 16. 'Fr Mathew Receives a Penitent Pledge Breaker', *c.* 1846, by James
Patrick Haverty (1794-1864). (National Gallery Ireland, Dublin)

Penitent Pledge Breaker', by Joseph Patrick Haverty (1794-1864)[45]
(Fig. 16). Internationally, there are also monuments to the memory
of Fr Mathew. For example, the Centennial Fountain, Fairmont,
Philadelphia, United States of America (Fig. 17). This was erected
under the auspices of the Catholic Total Abstinence Union of
America in honour of prominent Irish or Catholic Revolutionary
heroes. It was erected in 1875-77 by the National Temperance
Society at Fountain Avenue, Centennial Grounds, Philadelphia.
The monument, designed in the shape of a Maltese Cross, was created by Herman Kirn and contains statues of Fr Theobald Mathew
OSFC (Fig. 18), Charles Carroll (1737-1803) (the only Catholic
signatory to the Declaration of Independence), Commodore Barry
(1745-1803) (the Irish-born naval commander known as the father
of the American Navy) and Archbishop John Carroll (1735-1815)
(the founder of Georgetown University) mounted on fountain

pedestals. The central Moses sculpture rests upon a rock-mound within a marble basin with water flowing over the rocks into a pool.

Many biographies have been written about Fr Mathew over the years. Most have concentrated on his religious life, good works and the temperance movement. However, Fr Mathew's upbringing was different to most Irish Catholics and his seminary training was also different from that of Irish secular priests. In spite of his many achievements and his popularity with the general public of all creeds, both at home and abroad, he never gained the whole-hearted support of the bishops and clergy in Ireland. For example, he was an unsuccessful candidate to become Bishop of Cork in 1847 and he had little support from the Irish bishops for his temperance campaign. The prevailing view was that the temperance movement was utopian and impractical. In addition, he was perceived to have been too friendly with Protestant people, due to the closeness he had with his relatives, and with the British, as he had received a pension from the government.

In 2000, Cork Corporation proposed to move the Fr Mathew statue from its position on St Patrick's Street to a new location.

Fig. 17. The Centennial Fountain, Fairmount Park, Philadelphia, USA (erected in 1875-77). (Irish Capuchin Provincial Archives, Dublin)

Fig. 18.
Detail of the statue of
Fr Theobald Mathew
OSFC, Centennial
Fountain, Fairmount
Park, Philadelphia,
USA. (Irish Capuchin
Provincial Archives,
Dublin)

This idea was abandoned after protests from the people of Cork who regarded it as a landmark in its original location. This shows the continuing affection they have not only for 'the statue' but also for the memory of Fr Mathew.

4

Competition for the Initial Building of Holy Trinity Church

Of the many monuments built to commemorate Fr Mathew, the most significant is the building of Holy Trinity church in Cork City – the only church dedicated to his memory. The so-called 'wretched crib' in Blackamoor Lane had become too small for the large and over-flowing numbers that attended there. Just before the Catholic Emancipation Act of 1829, Fr Mathew decided to build a large and dignified place of worship for the people of Cork. The Act, which was largely the result of a campaign led by the Irish lawyer and MP Daniel O' Connell, also permitted Catholics to sit at Parliament in Westminster, something which had been denied to them for more than a hundred years.

As was the custom, a committee was set up to plan the building of the new church. A competition was held in 1825 and the committee awarded the contract, for £50, to the architect George R. Pain. The historian David Lee maintained that 'the brilliance of Pain's design for Holy Trinity was immediately apparent to virtually all those tasked with selecting a suitable design from among the nine architects' proposals submitted'.[46] The foundation stone was laid on 10 October 1832, which was also Fr Mathew's birthday. The occasion was a memorable one. It was the first time since the victory of

William III of England (1650-1702) – who was also known as the
Prince of Orange – that a Catholic ceremony, a religious procession
through the streets of the city, was held openly in Cork.[47]

In the early nineteenth century, Catholics were still circum-
scribed in the building of churches. Revd J. Coombes contended
that 'even with the erosion of the Penal Code, they still hesitated
to build steeples or belfries, not because the law forbade them but
because of a clause in the Relief Act of 1781-82'. This clause suggested that no benefit in the Act 'shall extend or be construed to
extend to any ecclesiastic who shall officiate in any church with a
steeple or bell'.[48] The design selected for Holy Trinity gave notice
that this new church, with its tall steeple and spire, was to be as
imposing as its non-Catholic neighbour churches.

The 1850s were marked by the large number of commissions
awarded for Catholic churches, schools and religious houses.
This was a phenomenon arising out of the granting of Catholic
Emancipation and, in the post-Famine years, this gathered momen-
tum.[49] The architectural historian Brendan Grimes affirmed that
'new church buildings would provide a focus for devotion, match
new formed morals and assert the right of Catholics to be as well
regarded as their Protestant neighbours'.[50]

George R. Pain and his brother James Pain (1777-1870) were
well-known architects in the city. Their father was a builder
in London and their grandfather was a writer on architecture.
They studied under the British Regency architect John Nash
(1752-1836) in London. He had designed, among other buildings, the Brighton Pavilion for the Prince Regent. They came to
Ireland in about 1811 to supervise the building of Lough Cutra
Castle, in County Galway. This had been designed by John Nash
for John Prendergast Smyth, the First Viscount Gort. James then
settled in Limerick and George in Cork and they worked together,
as well as separately[51] and built numerous houses all over Ireland,

notably Mitchelstown, County Cork, and Dromoland Castle, County Clare, in the style of John Nash. Coming from London, and having been associated with the Prince Regent's architect, would have given the Pains a certain *cachet*.

Their arch rivals were another set of architect brothers, Sir Thomas Deane (1772-1847) and Kearns Deane (1804-47). While Sir Thomas Deane worked in the realms of High Victorianism, for example his design for the Oxford Museum, the Pains remained firmly among the last of the Georgians.[52] In spite of the economic decline following the Act of Union, the first half of the nineteenth century was a period of great building activity in Ireland. This was particularly the case in the provinces, which benefitted from money and talent that would formerly have been drawn away by Dublin. The Pains and the Deanes were among the leaders of the Irish architectural profession.

The rivalry between the Pains and the Deanes is clear from a number of incidents, such as the commissions for the Holy Trinity and St Mary's (Dominican) churches. Deane's friend, the Irish antiquarian and folklorist Thomas Crofton Croker (1798-1854), was particularly partisan and wrote that 'the only buildings of merit in Cork were recent edifices built under the direction of Mr Thomas Deane'. He described the Pain's Blackrock Castle (1818-19) in Cork as 'a flimsy specimen of Cockney Gothic'. This was clearly a reference to the brothers' London origins.[53] The Pains' and the Deanes' paths were to cross many times in the construction of well-known buildings in Cork, including Holy Trinity church.

In 1832, when it became known that Fr Mathew planned to build a new church in Cork, a site was offered by the city authorities on Sullivan's Quay.[54] This site, opposite the Grand Parade, would have provided a much more dramatic location for the church. Instead, Fr Mathew decided to build it on Fr Mathew Quay (formerly Charlotte Quay).

There are differing stories about the reason for this decision, which also went against the wishes of his committee. One attributes it to a difference of opinion regarding what Fr Mathew considered to be an unreasonable demand from the owner of the Sullivan's Quay site. Another version is given by a relative of Mathew's, Mother Aloysius Nagle of the South Presentation Convent, who said that Fr Mathew wished to be located closer to the place where sailors could attend church. At that time, Charlotte Quay was one of the principal sites for loading and off-loading vessels in the city. Whatever the reason, the chosen site became the cause of delay and considerable additional expense as the site was marshy and had to be drained and piles driven far down into the ground. In addition, a special foundation had to be built to bear the heavy superstructure.[55] Steam engines had to be employed, night and day, to pump the water out. This cost nearly £1,600, before any portion of the church was built.[56]

Fig. 19. Etching of George R. Pain's original design for Holy Trinity church by
Mr J. O'Mahony which appeared in the *Irish Penny Magazine*, 1833.
(Irish Capuchin Provincial Archives, Dublin)

The estimated cost of building the church was £10,000. Some £5,000 was collected from 'generous citizens, both Catholic and Protestant' and Fr Mathew contributed £4,500 from his personal resources.[57] At the same time, two other substantial Catholic churches were being built in Cork City – St Mary's for the Dominican Order, designed by Sir Thomas Deane and his brother Kearns Deane, and St Patrick's, designed by George R. Pain for Bishop John Murphy. Fr Russell, of St Mary's, described the other two as 'our rival chapel builders'[58] as they would all have been trying to raise money from the same pool of people at a time of considerable poverty among Irish Catholics.

On 18 May 1833, the *Irish Penny Magazine* contained an etching, by Mr J. O'Mahony, of Pain's original design for the church (Fig. 19) and reported that:

> The beautiful edifice is now considerably in the process of being built on Charlotte Quay, in this city, under the inspection of T. Anthony Esq contracting architect, and according to a design by G.R. Pain Esq. The foundation stone was laid on the 23rd of last month.
>
> When completed, it will exhibit a pile of Gothic architecture, scarcely to be equalled for beauty and magnificence, within the Kingdom, and certainly most highly creditable to the well-known zeal and perseverance of the Very Rev. T. Mathew, and the religious reverence and liberality of the citizens of Cork. The church is of the Roman Catholic worship and is to be dedicated to the Holy Trinity. The interior will measure 128 by 60 feet, within the walls. It will be approached by three doorways all on the quay side. The edifice will be faced with cut stone, and the tower and spire, which will be elevated to the height of 182 feet, are to be of the same material. The total expense of its completion is

estimated at £12,000, the greater proportion of which is to be raised by public voluntary subscription, while a certain part has been, as I am led to understand, bequeathed for the purpose to the Very Rev gentleman named above.

The Irish Architectural Archive (IAA) in Merrion Square, Dublin has a wooden model of Pain's original design[59] (Fig. 20) which suggests that the etching in the *Irish Penny Magazine* was some-what exaggerated. The IAA also has a drawing by George R. Pain, from the Allen Collection, attributed as his original drawing for Holy Trinity church, Charlotte Quay, Cork (Fig. 21). This is clearly not the same church and is probably a drawing for the Protestant Christ Church (Holy Trinity), also in Cork, which was never executed.

Fig. 20.
A wooden model of George R. Pain's original design for Holy Trinity church, Cork. (Irish Architectural Archive, Dublin)

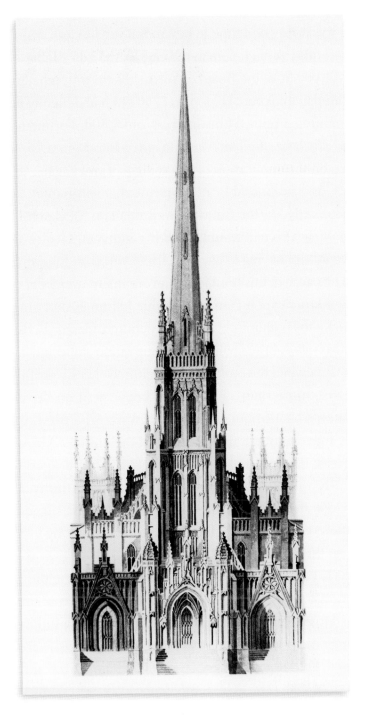

Fig. 21. A drawing by George R. Pain for Holy Trinity church
(Christ Church), Cork. (Allen Collection, Ballymaloe, County Cork)

1832 was not a good time to be fundraising in Cork as there was a serious outbreak of cholera in the city. In 1837, Fr Mathew had to borrow £1,000 from the Board of Works to help with relief works to cope with the epidemic. He repaid £250 but had difficulty meeting the remaining amount, plus interest, of £1,300. Fortunately, seventeen years later, the loan was converted into a grant.[60] This was achieved on the application of Mr William Trant Fagan (1801-59), MP for Cork, supported by other influential gentlemen, and the sum was remitted by the British Government on 31 March 1854.

Fr Mathew also had trouble with his architect, George R. Pain, resulting in him having to pay Pain £300 with costs following a lawsuit.[61] The cause of this trouble was an argument over 5 per cent on the expenditure which Pain felt was due to him as superintendent architect for the building of Holy Trinity church. George R. Pain died within five years of the laying of the foundation stone and Thomas Coakley supervised the building of the church after his death.

By 1840, more than £14,000 had been spent on the church, Fr Mathew's own financial resources were exhausted, the temperance movement engrossed him and the builder, Mr Anthony (*c.* 1798-1860), was unable to complete the building as he had apparently under-estimated his costs.[62] Mr Anthony alleged that he took the contract at too low a figure, at the suggestion of Fr Mathew, who privately guaranteed him against any loss. Work ceased on the building.[63]

In 1841, Fr Mathew said that he had not forgotten 'the church on Charlotte Quay and, when he had leisure to devote time to it, he hoped to complete the edifice independently of a shilling from the temperance cause'.[64] His best intentions, however, were not to be realised. Fr Mathew could not turn his attention to the unfinished church until such time as his temperance work was completed.

The Famine, and the devastation it caused, also had an effect on his work and activities and Fr Mathew was hard pressed to keep things going. On 29 June 1846, the Conservative government led by Sir Robert Peel (1788-1850) fell. This was due to political fallout over the repeal of the Corn Laws, which Peel had forced through Parliament. His departure paved the way for Charles Trevelyan (1807-86) to take full control of famine policy under the new Liberal government. The Liberals, led by Lord John Russell (1792-1878), were believers in the principle of *laissez-faire*.

Even though he was completely engrossed in famine relief work, Fr Mathew made time to correspond with Lord Trevelyan and wrote that 'in many places the wretched people were seated on the fences of their decaying gardens, wringing their hands and wailing bitterly the destruction that had left them food-less'.[65] In addition, Fr Mathew advocated food imports and soup kitchens rather than public works and other injections of cash. The latter had been the initial response of the government and had served only to drive up the price of available food.[66] In recognition of his work during the Famine period, Fr Mathew received a pension of £300 per annum from the government. The Prime Minister, Lord John Russell, had to overcome the reluctance of Queen Victoria who thought that Fr Mathew's work was 'by the aid of superstition which could hardly be patronised by the Crown'.[67]

In 1848, when the force of the Famine had subsided, a public meeting was held in Cork to recommence the building of Holy Trinity church. Weekly penny collections were held throughout the city and the first contribution for £5 'towards the completion of what ought to be a national monument' was acknowledged by Fr Mathew from Anne, Marchioness of Thomond, 'for the completion of his new church the works of which will recommence immediately'.[68] In 1850, Sir Thomas Deane, who had been an unsuccessful applicant for the original competition, was contracted to complete the church, without the portico and spire, and William Atkins (1812-87) was responsible for the church interior.[69]

It opened for worship on 10 October 1850. Fr Matthew was away in the United States of America, on temperance business, and was unable to attend.

The formal opening of Holy Trinity church was a magnificent affair. Admission was by ticket which cost 5s for a seat in the nave, 2s 6d for one in the aisle, and family tickets, to admit five persons, cost £1. A Pontifical High Mass was held on the day, including a performance of Beethoven's Mass in C, with full orchestra and a chorus of fifty voices. A public *dejeuner* for dignitaries was given in the Assembly Rooms and a grand procession was held through the streets of Cork. The consecrating prelate was Most Revd William Delany, Bishop of Cork, assisted by Most Revd Timothy Murphy, Bishop of Cloyne and Ross and Most Revd William Walsh, Bishop of Ossary. The sermon was preached by Dr O'Connell of Waterford. The religious services concluded with Romburg's *Te Deum*.

On the day of the opening, the grand procession through the city, consisted of the following:

Fig. 22. 'Daniel O'Connell Centenary in Dublin', *c.* 1890, by Charles Russell (1852-1910). (National Gallery Ireland, Dublin)

Tailors, engineers, iron-moulders, stone cutters, typo-
graphical, cork cutters, plasterers, sailors, firemen, dockers,
boiler-makers, port butchers, boot riveters, painters, building labourers, coopers, boot makers, plumbers, passage
shipwrights, bakers, masons, coach workers, farriers, gro-
cery workers, passage labourers, brewery workers, Cork
cabinet makers, gas workers, carpenters who were among
the groups of solidarities etc. who marched.[70]

This scene is reminiscent of a similar procession, depicted by the
artist Charles Russell (1852-1910) in 'The Daniel O'Connell
Centenary in Dublin', *c.* 1890 (Fig. 22),[71] which shows the banners
of different trade unions and others marching through the streets of
Dublin. Grimes described the opening of new Catholic churches
then as 'important social events, attended by many from the wealthy
and influential sections of society, indicating a general acceptance
of the role of Catholics in contributing to public architecture.[72]

5

Completion of Holy Trinity Church

Attempts were made to complete the church over succeeding years. For example, in about 1876, Fr Thomas Sheehy OSFC proposed to complete the front of the church by capping the pillars and erecting a tower. In June 1877, George Coppinger Ashlin (1837-1921), a Cork man who was a partner at the Dublin architectural firm of Pugin and Ashlin, came to Cork. His brother-in-law Edward Welby Pugin (1834-75), a son of A.W.N. Pugin, was is partner in the company. Ashlin inspected the foundation of the intended tower and made several sketch designs for the front, one of which was finally approved. The order was given for the working plans and for a new friary to be built afterwards in connection with it.[73] A lithograph, by H. Lane of 39 Dame Street, Dublin, depicted in a fundraising brochure for the completion of Holy Trinity church, shows the design which was selected from Pugin and Ashlin (Fig. 23). Had the building gone ahead at that time, it would have resulted in a complete deviation from Pain's original design for the front of the building. On 29 August 1877, Fr Sheehy resigned as Guardian in Cork. Perhaps this and/or a lack of funds resulted in the work not being carried out at that time.

On 28 December 1883, the *Freeman's Journal* drew attention to the deplorable state of the unfinished church and reported that 'the original design is a very beautiful one and, if carried out, would render the church exterior not as it is but a beautiful ornament to

PUGIN & ASHLIN ARCH??   J. LEWIS LITH. 29 DAME S? DUBLIN

DESIGN FOR THE COMPLETION OF THE CHURCH OF THE HOLY TRINITY – CORK.

COMMENCED BY THE LATE FATHER MATHEW – 1831

Fig. 23. Lithograph of Pugin & Ashlin's design for the completion of
Holy Trinity church, Cork. (Irish Capuchin Provincial Archives, Dublin)

Fig. 24. The exterior of Holy Trinity church, Cork before the portico and spire were added, *c.* 1870. (National Library of Ireland, Dublin)

the city'. As can be seen from a photograph of around 1865, Holy Trinity church was indeed in a desolate state at this stage (Fig. 24). It had the appearance of a barn and looked nothing like the graceful Gothic church that George R. Pain had originally designed, with its soaring portico and spire.

Fr Paul Neary OSFC (d. 1939), from Freshford, County Kilkenny, was one of the youngest Superiors appointed to the Capuchin Order in Ireland. In 1890, he organised the celebrations for Fr Mathew's centenary in Cork. He is also credited with the expansion of the Order in Ireland, as well as the successful completion of Holy Trinity church by the addition of the spire and portico. On 24 February 1889, Fr Neary opened an inaugural meeting in Cork in an attempt to complete the church to mark the centenary of Fr Mathew's birth.[74] The patrons were Cardinal Henry E. Manning (1808-92), Archbishop of Westminster (1868-92) and Sir Wilfred Lawson MP (1829-1906). The latter said that 'a sober Ireland would be the noblest monument which can be raised to his memory'. Fr Mathew was reputed to have said, 'the church is not finished, but it will be finished after my death'. The purpose of the meeting was to fulfil his prophecy. Mr Timothy Michael Healy MP (1855-1931) added that 'Fr Mathew was a great ecclesiastic and a great social reformer'. They decided to complete the church according to the original design by George R. Pain, as a fitting tribute to Fr Mathew.

Fr Neary described the unfinished church as 'a longstanding eyesore in the middle of a great cathedral city'. He went on to say that 'a stain had besmirched our own Capuchin Order in the public mind, for having left the church unfinished for nearly forty years'.[75]

Not unusually, when a church is finished to the extent that it satisfies the needs of religious observance, people tend to lose interest in its final completion. The completion of the church was also a controversial issue as the Bishop of Cork, Very Revd T. O'Callaghan OP (1886-1916), was worried that people in Ireland and in the United States of America would not support the fundraising drive.[76] This would add to the burden of ordinary citizens in Cork. The church building committee, therefore, had to ensure that they had the support of the public, both at home and abroad, so as to collect enough money for the project.

A leaflet advertising a competition to complete the façade of the church was issued by the committee and signed by Mr Denny

Lane MA (1818-95), chairman. It stated that it 'should embrace the pillars already built' and 'the cost not to exceed £6,000' and that 'the facing of all the work should be of chiselled limestone, to correspond with the present building'. The leaflet went on to say that 'to three which they deem most suitable, they [the committee] would award a premium of £50 to the author'. From these three designs, the Building Committee, in consultation with their architect, 'will then select the one which seems to them the best, subject to the approval of the Committee'.

The *Irish Builder*[77] reported that, of the twelve sets of proposals submitted in 1889, the consultant architect, Mr G.C. Ashlin of the Dublin firm of Pugin & Ashlin, recommended a design by Walter G. Doolin as being the most suitable. Instead, the committee choose to award the contract to Dominick J. Coakley (d. 1914), a local man. Coakley added the portico and spire but on a reduced scale to the original design by George R. Pain. Coakley is probably related to Thomas Coakley who supervised the original building of the church. The architect Jeremy Williams said that the committee, in its selection of Coakley, had made 'a fortunate choice as, apart from reducing the spire, he realised Pain's intentions'.[78] The reduced height of the spire was probably due to continuing problems with the foundations. It was a difficult and exacting task as shown in a photograph of around 1890, depicting the work in progress of completing the portico and steeple, on the western façade of the church, under Coakley's supervision (Fig. 25). This shows the tall, complex and delicate wooden scaffolding that had to be used in its construction.

It is interesting to note that the stone for the spire and portico came from the same quarry as that used for the original building. The quarry belonged to a man called Cantillon of Little Island, just outside the city. Cantillon never allowed stone from that area of the quarry to be used until work on the church recommenced,

Fig. 25. Construction work on the portico and spire of Holy Trinity church,
Cork, *c.* 1890. (Irish Capuchin Provincial Archives, Dublin)

nearly forty years later.[79] This ensured the uniformity of colour in the whole of the building.

From the outset, the site chosen by Fr Mathew was a costly mistake. Before commencing the spire and portico an excavation had to be made in front of the pillars of the original church to gauge their state of preservation. Fr Neary noted that:

> The opening revealed that the pillars stand on a solid wall of masonry, 21ft. deep and 5ft. thick, built with inverted arches and resting upon piles. A corresponding north wall of masonry and arches bind together the pillars and the front wall and again that wall to the pillars under, for the purpose of bracing and consolidating the whole façade.[80]

Notwithstanding all that, a subsidence had occurred under the façade that cast doubt on the capacity of the foundations to support the spire. Today, in the organ gallery, one can see strong, square iron bars connecting the inside pillars with the main wall. They were inserted at the time and used as ties to mutually strengthen the pillars and wall and hold them in place.[81] When opened, Fr Neary noted that the foundations were found to be perfect but 'one of the unsupported pillars was five-eighths of an inch out of plumb'. The architects did not consider this to be a serious defect as long as the super-structure was to be light. It is likely that the original height of George R. Pain's original spire was reduced in the interests of safety and stability.

The *Cork Examiner* of 29 August 1891 reported that:

> The work of completion of the Fr Mathew Memorial Church is now all but completed … It is a worthy memorial of its renowned patron which is admired by all who have seen it. To Mr D.J. Coakley, as conceiver of the design,

and Mr J. Sisk its builder, the work is in the highest degree creditable...The style is Gothic English of perpendicular type. The façade consists of a portico of three arches, the full height of the arches, with screens of sculptured stone work at the base and niches containing figures of the patron saints and martyrs. The general principle being mindful of Peterborough Cathedral save that the central arch is much wider than the high arches. Over the main gable rises the tower which rests on the piers of the centre posts. It is in these stages reducing in width as it ascends and the angles of each stage are marked with pinnacles and flying buttresses. The novel feature of the design is the treatment of the angles which are of peculiar strength. The spire is octagonal and it is also supported by flying buttresses at the angles and is heightened by lofty hurricane windows. A cross of wrought iron adorns the whole and

Fig. 26. The porch of Holy Trinity church, Cork. The heads on either side of the portico were carved by John Hogan (1800-58). (Clodagh Evelyn Kelly, Dublin)

points to about the height of 160 feet. The whole design is exceedingly graceful.

The carved heads on either side of the church door, in the porch, were made by the eminent Irish sculptor John Hogan, who was paid £10 for this work.[82] There are two statues, one above the other, on either side of the main archway, including St Anthony of Padua and St Claire (Fig. 26). A statue is also placed on the walls, at either side of the main portico, which are now somewhat weather worn. Williams also praised the exquisite carvings on Pain's façade which he said resembled Coolclough church.[83]

Mr Denny Lane, a Young Irelander and chairman of the committee, expressed grave doubts as to whether they would be able to complete the church on time. He said that such a fortune would be 'nothing short of a national disgrace'. The Young Irelanders were influenced by the inter-denominational ideals of Theobald Wolfe Tone (1763-98) and the United Irishmen of the 1790s. Wolfe Tone was a leading Irish revolutionary and founder of the United Irishmen.

The church was finally completed and opened on 13 October 1890 to much fanfare and, by all accounts, it was a most impressive and momentous occasion. Entrance to this opening of the church was also by ticket, nave 5s, eastern aisle 2s 6d and western aisle 1s 1d. The full amount received on the day was £72.[84] On 10 October 1890, an advertisement in the *Cork Examiner* informed the public that the inaugural ceremony, to celebrate the first day of the Fr Mathew centenary celebrations, would include a *dejeuner* in the Assembly Rooms, a reception in the School of Art and an orchestral concert.

6

Architectural Context of Holy Trinity Church

George R. Pain's design for Holy Trinity church is in the English Gothic Revival style. The architectural historian Matthew McDermott contended that the Gothic Revival was introduced into Ireland, from England, during the first half of the nineteenth century, although some forerunners were already in Ireland. For example, John Semple (*c.* 1763-*c.* 1841) designed the Chapel Royal in Dublin Castle in 1807 and executed the building in a very fine Gothic decorative style. Semple's churches, however, were designed with a view to economy. His simplified style of medieval architecture was much cheaper to build than the classical. This simple style was also used by the Pains of Cork.[85]

The Gothic style emphasises verticality and light which is achieved by architectural features such as clustered columns, ribbed vaults and flying buttresses. Augustus Welby Northmore Pugin (1812-52) was the most important figure in the history of the Gothic Revival. He was taught by his father who had worked in the office of John Nash. He attempted to justify Gothic architecture as the basis of objective principles and wrote many influential books on this topic.[86] The most famous are *The True Principles of Pointed or Christian Architecture* (1841) and *The Glossary of*

Ecclesiastical Ornament (1884), which were widely read. He sub-
jected architecture to more analysis which established Gothic as a
suitable style for modern buildings, particularly churches.

The nineteenth century was the great church building period
in Irish history. Catholics were by then allowed to build churches,
and did so on an impressive scale, and Protestants of all denomi-
nations were determined to keep up. The architectural historian
Megan Aldrich argued that the Gothic style of the eighteenth
century 'had strong associations with Medieval Catholics which
were furthered in the nineteenth century by the writings of
A.W.N. Pugin. Catholic patrons were to occupy a prominent position in the Gothic Revival'.[87]

Pugin also worked in Ireland. For example, he designed
Killarney Cathedral (1847) and Enniscorthy Cathedral (1840)
which are major examples of early Gothic Revival in Ireland.

Holy Trinity church is made of light grey limestone and the
tower and spire are about 160 feet in height. This is shorter than
the original design by Pain, which was to have been 182 feet in
height (Fig. 27). The portico has three very high arches, which
are on octagonal piers. There is a stone screen between the piers,
forming a porch for the central doorway. There are ten columns at
the angles of the building. The columns not connected with the
tower terminate, with flying buttresses springing externally from
them. Similar buttresses are used in the turrets, at the angles of the
tower, which rise from above these arches. The tower consists of
two storeys, has an open parapet of tracery passing around it, and
the spire rising above. The upper story of the tower and the lower
portion of the spire are open (Fig. 28). The church has Gothic
arched windows, with curvilinear cusped tracery and hood mouldings, a four-centred arched doorway, hood mouldings on corbels
carved with masks, and twinned doors with over-panels which
have quatrefoil glazed panels.

Fig. 27. The exterior of Holy Trinity church, Cork with portico and steeple.
(Clodagh Evelyn Kelly, Dublin)

George R. Pain's design is in a more simplified Gothic style, albeit with its characteristic spiky quality. The writer and co-founder of the *Irish Arts Review*, Brian de Breffni, observed that 'Pain abandoned his customary restrained Gothic in his unusual portico for the Holy Trinity church in Cork'.[88] It is thought that Pain was influenced in this by the design of Peterborough Cathedral, Cambridgeshire, England (Fig. 29) although the central arch in Holy Trinity church is much higher than the side arches. The architectural historian Dr Christine Casey suggested that St Augustine and John's church (1863-99), Thomas Street, Dublin also 'recalls the great arched portals of Peterborough Cathedral'.[89] However, St Augustine and John's has a more chiselled design (Fig. 30) when compared to Holy Trinity church. The latter is more graceful and spiky which enhances the illusion of height and lightness. Coincidently, Ashlin and Coleman, the architects who designed the St Augustine and

Fig. 28.
The spire of Holy
Trinity church,
Cork, c. 1960.
(Irish Capuchin
Provincial Archives,
Dublin)

Fig. 29. Peterborough Cathedral, Cambridgeshire, England. (Peterborough Cathedral)

John's church, were also commissioned to carry out an extension to Holy Trinity church, Cork in 1908.

Casey argued that Dublin churches from 1815 to 1850, with few exceptions, were mostly 'essays in Greek and Roman Neo-Classicism'.[90] While the design for Holy Trinity church is Gothic, the Pains were amenable to many architectural styles. David Lee suggested that 'unlike Pugin, the Pains were not ideologically committed to any one style of architecture – Classical or Gothic'.[91] For example, the design for St Patrick's church in Cork, by George R. Pain, is Classical. The Pains were probably more likely to suit the style of the day and to satisfy the taste of their clients.

The greatest High Victorian Gothic building in Cork, or arguably anywhere in Britain and Ireland, is the magnificent St Finbarr's Cathedral (1865-79), designed by Sir William Burges (1827-81). The art historian Dr Michael J. Lewis, described it as the 'finest cathedral designed under the influence of Ecclesiology'.[92] The design of this Church of Ireland cathedral was clearly making a statement by virtue of its size and location. Nevertheless, while

Fig. 30.
St Augustine and
John's church, John's
Lane, Thomas Street,
Dublin. (Courtesy of
Irish Augustinian
Order, Dublin)

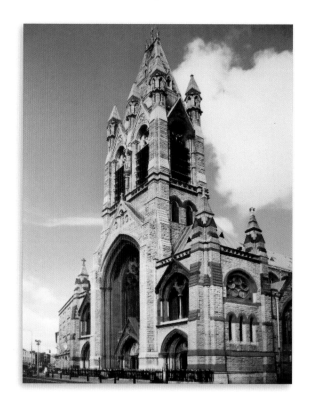

it is not on an elevated site, Holy Trinity church occupies its own
unique place on the Cork City skyline. During the nineteenth
century, Catholic and Protestant patrons were equally important
in the commissioning of architects to design new churches and
cathedrals in Ireland. They both embraced many styles, including
the Gothic Revival, whether the latter was in the simpler form of
Pain or the more elaborate style of Burges.

The Gothic Revival was probably an antidote to the modernism
of the Industrial Revolution. Nevertheless, as in other countries,
the growing use of new building materials, such as cast-iron, was also
a factor in early nineteenth-century Ireland. Edward Dieselkamp
contended that two issues encouraged the adoption of this new
building material. These were an interest in fire-resistant materials
and construction methods and an interest in novel ways to admit
natural light into buildings and greenhouses.[93] He further argued

that the use of cast-iron 'was applicable to all styles of architecture ... cast-iron could be moulded and cast in identical proportions to imitate stone'. [94] This was particularly useful for Gothic mouldings and tracery. Thomas Rickman (1776-1841), a British-based Gothic Revival architect, used cast-iron for moulded decorative castings in many of his churches, instead of carved stone. St George's church, Everton, Liverpool (1813-14) is a good example of this work. However, there was a suspicion of modern materials. Lewis noted that in 1851, the leading English art critic John Ruskin (1819-1900) described the Crystal Palace as 'a fanciful greenhouse'. [95] This was constructed for the first International Exhibition held in London in 1850. However, the arguments against cast-iron soon collapsed and Lewis went on to say that 'Deane and Woodward's constructed iron museum gallery at Oxford won begrudging acceptance, even from Ruskin'. [96]

Stephen Parissien contended that Nash was not the only Regency champion of iron construction. Humphrey Repton (1752-1818), a master English landscape designer, advocated the use of iron 'not just to mimic more traditional materials and dispositions but to create many beautiful effects of lightness'. [97] These qualities were enthusiastically exploited by the architects of new industrial buildings, who utilised cast-iron columns to create large, spacious and well-lit areas. An early example of cast-iron work in Ireland is the graceful Ha'penny Bridge which was built over the River Liffey in Dublin in 1816. [98] Other examples are Irish railway stations, such as Heuston (formerly Kingsbridge Station) in Dublin and Ceannt (formerly Glanmire Road Station) in Cork.

Holy Trinity church has cast-iron columns, which give an airy feel to its high-ceilinged interior. However, when they were first introduced, the congregation did not appreciate the starkness of the cast-iron and the columns were covered over with thick wooden casings (Fig. 31). During renovations in the 1980s, they were again exposed, but the

Fig. 31. The former thick wooden casings on the cast-iron columns in Holy Trinity
church, Cork, 1960s. (Courtesy of Professor Douglas Richardson, Toronto, Canada)

congregation reacted in the same way and today they are re-covered in
narrow wooden casings (Fig. 32).

Only a few uncovered original cast-iron columns are visible
today, for example in the porch of the church. The columns were
made by McSwiney's of Cork. This foundry was opened in 1816
by Paul McSwiney in MacCurtain Street (formerly King Street).
Also known as the King Street Iron Works, the firm was in
operation until the early years of the twentieth century. *Cork
Industries – Past and Present* noted that 'as long ago as 1840, it is
recorded that there were in existence in Cork at least nine iron
and brass foundries doing good work'. The cast-iron columns in
the porch area are considerably smaller than those in the main
body of the church. It has not been possible to confirm that both
were made by McSwiney's of Cork nor if the company had the
physical capacity to cast the much larger columns.

The cast-iron columns in the church have been covered over
for so long that some people have forgotten about their origin.

Fig. 32.
Today's slim wooden casings
on the cast-iron columns
of Holy Trinity church,
Cork, 2014. (Clodagh
Evelyn Kelly, Dublin)

For example, in his description of the church, Jeremy Williams stated that the original interior had been destroyed 'due to a drastic modernisation of recent years that has replaced the original arcades with slender steel supports to improve the sight lines from the aisles'.[99] As noted above, this is not a correct interpretation of what happened, as the columns are made of cast-iron which were subsequently re-covered in wooden casings.

Holy Trinity church represents an early example of the use of cast-iron in a church building in Ireland and it is probable that cast-iron was used due to the difficulties encountered in laying its foundations on marshy land. Cast-iron columns would have been a considerably lighter weight-bearing material compared to stone columns.

7

Building the Capuchin Friary

Following the closure of their residence on Blackamore Lane in around 1850, the Capuchins occupied various houses in different locations in Cork City, as dictated by political circumstance and whatever accommodation was available to them. On 10 June 1866, the *Cork Examiner* reported that 'a foundation stone for a new convent for the Capuchin Friars in the city was laid yesterday by Revd P. Timmons, immediately adjoining the church of the Holy Trinity on Charlotte Quay'. It is likely that the Superior of the Order was anxious to have a new building that would bring the Capuchin Friars together in one place.

It was decided to avail of the limited surplus grounds around the church as a site. The *Cork Examiner* further reported that 'Mr John Hurley, the clever and respected architect of this city, offered his services for free'. An 1841 Ordnance Survey map[100] shows the probable location of the friary built around the northern and part of the western perimeters of the church (Fig. 33). Today, one can still see a bricked-up door on the wall at the side entrance to the church from Fr Mathew Street (formerly Queen Street), which was probably part of the entrance to this early friary (Fig. 34).

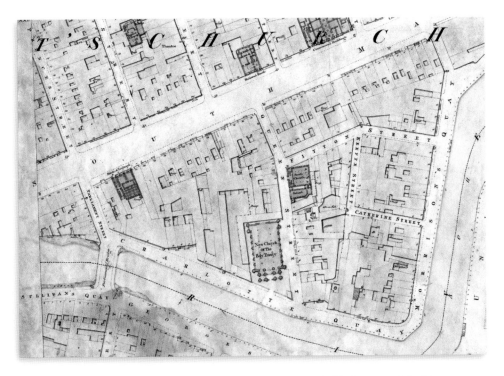

Fig. 33. Plan of Holy Trinity church, Cork, showing probable location of the friary built around some of its perimeter. (National Archives of Ireland (NAI), OS 140/41 Cork City – sheet 23 – scale 1:1056 (year 1841). National Archives of Ireland, Dublin)

The present-day friary was built in 1884 by the architect Robert Walker (*c.* 1835-1910). On 10 June 1884, the *Cork Examiner* reported that:

> The new convent is a beautiful structure, rectangular in shape, three stories high and built entirely of limestone. The style of the architecture is Domestic Gothic, designed by Mr Walker and built by Mr Delany. The front borders on Charlotte Quay and is almost in line with the façade of the church, close to which it stands. The appearance of the building is quite in keeping with its noble purpose and, viewed from the opposite side of the river, the edifice produced is pleasing in the extreme.

However, Williams is not quite as enthusiastic as he described the adjoining friary as 'a robust but crude design in Ballintemple limestone, banded with red brick, jammed up against the church by Robert Walker in 1888'.[101] On 5 July 1884, the *Cork Daily Herald* also commented on the same building and reported that:

> Robert Walker, architect, drew up plans for a building which combines solidarity, convenience and beauty with a simplicity and harmony of design. It introduces features of architecture which are new to Cork. The architect seems to have studied the Continental style with extreme care and has brought the result to bear upon the new building in a manner deserving the highest praise, indicating his familiarity with the features of the monasteries on the Continent in Germany and France and even in Rome.

Fig. 34.
The bricked-up doorway
at the Fr Mathew Street
(formerly Queen Street) entrance
to Holy Trinity church, Cork.
(Clodagh Evelyn Kelly, Dublin)

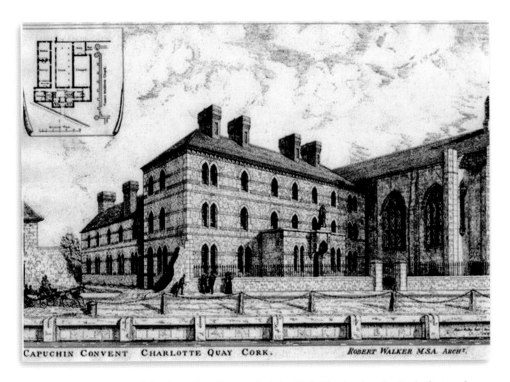

CAPUCHIN CONVENT CHARLOTTE QUAY CORK. ROBERT WALKER M.SA. ARCH^T.

Fig. 35. Engraving of the Capuchin Friary, adjoining Holy Trinity church, Cork, designed
by Robert Walker (c. 1835-1910). (Irish Capuchin Provincial Archives, Dublin)

It is hard to reconcile these differing views on the Capuchin Friary
in Cork other than to suggest that they are probably dictated by taste.
In essence, it is a Venetian Gothic style building that is rather plain
and functional looking, located at the side of the church. It is built
around a quadrangle and has an enclosed garden at the back of the
building. Its design is also probably an antidote to its more elaborate
neighbour, Holy Trinity church itself, and is more in keeping with
the spirit of simplicity of the Capuchin Order (Fig. 35). This etching, which appeared in *The Architect* on the 24 February 1880, also
highlights the incomplete state of Holy Trinity church at the time.
In 1934, a statue of St Francis was erected over the entrance to the
friary. This was executed by John Power and was donated by members of the Third Order.

8

Stained-Glass Windows in Holy Trinity Church

There are some very interesting, albeit relatively unknown, stained-glass windows in Holy Trinity church that, to date, have not been investigated to any extent. Due to renovations over the years, which have completely altered the interior of the church, the stained-glass windows are its most interesting remaining interior features. There is also a great variety of style and design in these windows which range from the mid-1800s to the early 1900s.

The first mention of a stained-glass window dates back to 1848 when £320 was collected by the citizens of Cork for a fitting memorial to Daniel O'Connell 'The Liberator', who had died the previous year. The committee involved decided that the money should be used for the erection of a monumental window in Fr Mathew's Chapel.[102] This was a controversial decision at the time as most people expected a public statue to have been commissioned to commemorate O'Connell. The window was designed by Isaac Alexander Gibbs Snr (1802-51) who founded the stained-glass company of I.A. Gibbs and Co., based in Hampstead Road, London.[103] I.A. Gibbs Snr had seven sons, three of whom became stained-glass artists. I.A. Gibbs Snr exhibited at the Great Exhibition of 1851, held at Crystal Palace in Hyde Park,

Fig. 36. O'Connell Memorial Window by I.A. Gibbs & Co., London,
Holy Trinity church, Cork. (Clodagh Evelyn Kelly, Dublin)

London. One of his better-known commissions is in the south
nave of Ely Cathedral in Firth.[104]

The O'Connell Memorial Window cost £525 and was installed
in 1850 (Fig. 36).[105] It has four lights with five panels in each.
The main theme, which is depicted on the second and fourth rows,
illustrates eight different episodes from The Life of Christ. These
are, from top to bottom and from left to right, 'The Annunciation',
'The Adoration of the Wise Men', 'Christ Disputing with the
Doctors in the Temple', 'The Baptism of Christ', 'The Last
Supper', 'The Crucifixion', 'The Ascension' and 'The Day of
Pentecost'. On the first, third and fifth rows of the window are

depictions of the four evangelists, Matthew, Mark, Luke and John, in the Ezekiel symbols (Angel, Lion, Ox and Eagle), as well as the head of St Francis, the arms of the Capuchin Order, angels and other symbols. All of these scenes and symbols are framed by illuminated borders of flowers and vines in brilliant colours of red, yellow and blue. At the top of the window is a representation of the Holy Trinity and underneath are the Virgin, on the right, and Christ, on the left-hand side. Below them are four trefoils, with a depiction of an angel in each. There is an inscription at the base, in illuminated characters of yellow on a black background, spread across all four lights, which reads:

> Sacred in gratitude and affection to the memory of Daniel O'Connell, the Liberator of his fellow Catholics from the Penal Code, and asserter of the equal right of all commun-ions to civil and religious freedom RIP.

At the base of the window are the O'Connell family crest, on the left-hand side, and the signature of the maker, 'I.A. Gibbs, *Pinx* London', on the right-hand side. Br Benvenutus Dortmans OSFC of Rotterdam gave an unusual endorsement to the window when he said that 'Mr Gibbs reputation as an artist would but be slightly enhanced by anything we could say'.[106]

This imposing window is the first thing that strikes one on entry to the church, with its rich primary colours of red, blue and yellow. It is a typical Victorian-style window, with strong textured borders framing individual scenes. It is also an impressive window due to its sheer size, almost filling the northern gable wall in the sanctuary area behind the main altar. It is important too as it is the only memorial in Cork City to Daniel O'Connell. The 1851 edition of *Battersby's Catholic Registry* said that 'this beautiful monument reflects equal credit on the skill of the artist and the good taste of the committee'. [107]

There are two windows in the church that appear to have been made by the same stained-glass artist, as identical motifs appear at the top of each. They each depict a harp on a grey/blue background. There is a trefoil above each harp containing a flower at the centre and what look like pelicans on either side. There is also a *fleur de lis* motif on the background tile-like squares of both windows.

The first is a small square window that is situated high on the western wall of the church, directly above the friar's gallery. It depicts the *Coat of Arms of Pope Leo XIII* (1878-1903), which is the main subject of the window (Fig. 37). Surrounding the crest is written '*In Memorium Leo XIII Lumen in Coelo, Pontifex Maximus*' and the inscription at the bottom reads 'In memory … O'Connor' The first name is illegible but it is known that the O'Connor family were benefactors of the church.

The second is a beautiful single lancet window, directly above the side entrance to the church, from Father Mathew Street (formerly Queen Street), on the eastern wall. It is a depiction of the 'Immaculate Conception' (Fig. 38). The Virgin is standing on a pinkish globe and a green red-headed serpent, under a golden ornate and sculptured form of canopy. She is wearing a blue cape over a plain robe and her sash and the borders of her cape are very decorative. Her halo is also relatively plain in design. All are placed above what appears to be a golden shrine which is also sculptured and architectural in its design. There are multi-colour shell-like motifs above this shrine. The Virgin is surrounded by striking purple and yellow striped beams that emanate from behind her figure. The inscription at the bottom reads 'In memory of Matthew Honan, benefactor of this church'. This is the same Matthew Honan who is commemorated by the Honan Chapel at University College, Cork (UCC) and who died in 1907.

The stained-glass artist is unknown and there are no marks on either window to help with their identification. It is thought that the artist was from Glasgow and was possibly called Hemmings.[108]

The only Hemmings with a Scottish connection that could be found that fits in with the dates is Alfred Octavius Hemmings (1843-1907) of A.O. Hemmings and Co. He trained as an architect in Edinburgh and, in 1868, joined Clayton and Bell as a stained-glass artist. In 1883, he set up his own stained-glass studio at 47 St Margaret's Street, London and later at 2 Nottingham Terrace, York Gate, Marylebone Road, London where his firm continued, under Robert H. Corbould, until 1930.[109] According to the British Society of Master Glass Producers, he may also have worked in Newcastle. While Hemming's career corresponds with the installation of these windows, and his sculptured and architectural style fit the design, there is no indication that he was the artist.

Three windows, which were added to the church at a later date, are of great Irish interest. They were created by the studio of J. Clarke and Sons and designed by Harry Clarke (1889-1931) of Dublin. Harry Clarke (Fig. 39) was born in Dublin and, during his short life, he was one of the first indigenous stained-glass artists to achieve international recognition. He was also a renowned

Fig. 37.
O'Connor Memorial Window,
Holy Trinity church, Cork.
(Clodagh Evelyn Kelly, Dublin)

Fig. 38. Honan Memorial Window,
Holy Trinity church, Cork.
(Clodagh Evelyn Kelly, Dublin)

graphic artist. In 1858, his father, Joshua Clarke (*c.* 1868-1921), came to Ireland from Leeds and established a church decorating and stained-glass business on North Frederick Street, Dublin. Harry was educated at Belvedere College, Dublin (1896-1903) and, on leaving school, joined the family business, as did his brother, Walter Clarke (*c.* 1887-1930). He studied at night at the Metropolitan School of Art in Dublin (1905-10) and, for a short period, at the National Art Training School in Kensington, London (1906). In three successive years he won the gold medal for stained glass in the national competition organised by the Board of Education (1911-13), and was the first ever Irish student awarded top prize in this genre. In 1914 he married Margaret Crilly (1888-1961), who was also a renowned artist, and they had three children.[110] In 1914, Harry was awarded a travelling scholarship, by the Department of Agriculture and Technical Instruction, and he used this to study stained glass in France. He was influenced by the medieval glass he saw during this time and by Continental artists such as Aubrey Beardsley (1872-95), and this is evident in his work. However, he developed his own unique style, with its exquisite drawing detail as well as jewel-like colours, and succeeded in adapting modern European art to an Irish style.

In 1913, Harry Clarke illustrated his first series of books, for Harraps of London, which established his reputation as an illustrator. His first large-scale stained-glass commission was in 1915 when he completed eleven windows for the Honan Chapel at University College, Cork (UCC). This firmly established his reputation as a stained-glass artist. Thomas Bodkin (1887-1961), Director of the National Gallery of Ireland (1927-35), remarked that nothing like these windows had been produced in Ireland and that the 'beautiful and most intricate drawing, the lavish and mysterious symbolism, combine to produce an effect of splendour which is overpowering'.[111]

Following the success of these windows, Harry had no shortage of commissions and he was also in demand as an illustrator of books. He was a notoriously hard worker and, even though he was not in good health, took on more commissions than he could comfortably handle. When his father died in 1921, he and his brother Walter took

Fig. 39. Self-portrait ink drawing by Harry Clarke (1889-1931). (Collection: Dublin City Gallery – The Hugh Lane, Dublin)

over the running of his studio, even though Harry continued with his own private commissions as well. By the time of his brother's death in 1930, he had established his own company – Harry Clarke Stained Glass Studio Limited. Due to overwork, a serious bicycle accident and continuing poor health he had to go to Switzerland in 1929 for treatment. He died there during his second visit in 1931.[112]

The *Cork Examiner* of 8 January 1982 noted that one of the treasures of Holy Trinity church was 'the Harry Clarke stained glass windows on the eastern side of the church'. These three large windows have also been described as priceless. They are windows of sheer beauty and a superb example of Clarke's art. None of these windows, however, are mentioned in the *Gazeteer of Irish Stained Glass*. Originally the windows were located in the sanctuary area but, after major renovation work in the 1980s, they were re-located to the nave, in the main body of the church. This location shows off their brilliance to great effect, particularly in the morning light, and provides a very pleasing triptych effect. While they are sited together, they were commissioned at different times, and by different patrons.

The first of these three large windows was commissioned just after the First World War. In the early 1900s, Ireland was a country in turmoil, divided by the issue of Home Rule. Irish Nationalists saw their goal within reach whereas Unionists, led by Dubliner Lord Edward William Carson (1854-1936), prepared for resistance by force. Against this background, violent industrial conflicts were also taking place. Prices were soaring and wages were not keeping pace and there were many strikes in Dublin, Cork and elsewhere for higher wages. Fr Thomas Dowling OSFC (1874-1951), who had studied social reform, established the first Conciliation Board in Cork and became an arbitrator and mediator between employers and trade unions.[113] As a result, the Cork and District Trades and Labour Council decided to donate a window to Holy Trinity church, in appreciation of the work Fr Dowling had carried out. Harry Clarke had just completed, to great acclaim, his stained-glass windows for the Honan Chapel at UCC.[114] Probably due to this, the commission for the Fr Thomas Dowling Memorial Window was given to Clarke. Coincidently, Mr James F. McMullan (1859-1933) was the architect for both the Honan Chapel and Holy Trinity church.

Problems arose in this commission, which resulted in a lengthy correspondence between Harry Clarke and the architect. On 20 June 1918, Harry wrote to McMullan arguing that 'I cannot be bound in any way to the drawing ... I cannot promise that the inscription will be readable from the ground. You might again consider the quotation of the tablet in case anyone might want to know what the long written matter in the window was all about'.[115] The Cork and District Trades and Labour Council wished to have a very long inscription incorporated into the window. Harry's point was that such a large inscription could not be read from the ground and, undoubtedly, would also detract from the overall artistic impact of the window. On 9 July 1918, Harry again wrote to McMullan in an effort to break the impasse 'I aim to meet you on the question of the Union'.[116]

A further problem appeared in a letter to McMullan on 12 August 1918, when Harry wrote:

> I have only now been able to look at the Trades' window which were sent to me by Sisk ... I find the actual size of the window exceeds the size you gave me and of which I have your tracing ... Let me know what your Committee proposes to do as I can hardly be expected to do this extra work for nothing.[117]

Dr Nicola Gordon Bowe, in her definitive biography on the life and work of Harry Clarke, said that 'the actual size of the window exceeded McMullan's original size and that the committee were trying to include a crucifixion in the design for the same price'.[118] Naturally, Harry was not willing to do the window unless the patrons agreed to pay him for this extra work. Sir John R. O'Connell (1868-1943), a well-known philanthropist and solicitor and an activist in Irish cultural life, was called in to mediate. He agreed with Harry Clarke's argument.[119] The issue of an additional payment was reiterated again in a letter of 28 September 1918, from Harry to McMullan, 'may I remind you that the windows at Holy Trinity church measure twenty square foot more than the sizes you originally gave me ... Unless the donors will pay me for this extra work I cannot do this window'.[120]

By 26 September 1918, things came to a head and Harry, who had become totally disaffected with the project, wrote to McMullan:

> I do not intend proceeding with the window for £250 ... There is no problem me withdrawing from the original agreement ... It simply means that your clients will not pay me for the extra work in addition to what I agreed to do for the above sum ... If I had to pay £50 for extra materials on a job on which I had already dropped twenty ... I take it for granted that the matter is now closed between us and in conclusion offer a solution i.e I will give my design to the Studio here, will select the glass and generally supervise your window. In this way you would be sure of a good window for the money at your disposal – but the window will not be mine though this fact will not I am sure trouble your clients very much.[121]

On 2 November 1918, Joshua Clarke, who was very keen to take on his son Harry's commission, wrote to Fr Thomas Dowling OSFC at Holy Trinity church:

I understand that there is some quibbling as such in relation to your church in Cork … I think it would be as well
if it would be all the same to you to hand this window over
to me. I will give you as good work as you would get my son
or anyone else. It will not be the same style as my son's but
it will be as good in quality and execution. I will take the
window at the price of £250 and I will guarantee to have it
fixed in its place within five months. As regards inscription,
which I believe there was some words about, I can arrange
that in discussing the window to suit whatever inscription
you like. I hope Fr Thomas that you will be able to use your
influence to ask the architect to give the order to me.[122]

Fr Thomas seems to have persuaded the architect to take on this
suggestion as the next correspondence is from Joshua Clarke to
McMullan on 8 November 1918. Joshua affirmed that he would
take on the commission to his own design, as he did not think
it would be fair to ask his son, Harry, for his drawings since he
was not going to benefit from the work. He also confirmed that
when Harry said that 'it would not be my work' he only meant that
he would not be working directly on the window himself. Joshua
went on to give the patrons a choice: 'I have included a descriptive
specification of my son's design and, if this suits, it would not be
necessary to get out a further design.'[123]

A letter from Joshua to McMullan, on 11 November 1918, confirmed that the commission had been given 'we have received your
favour of the 8th inst'.[124] The original Order No. 1090 was received on
27 November 1918, to be fitted by 27 April 1919, to 'design supply
and fit memorial windows Holy Trinity church, Cork as per letter
and agreement at a cost of £250'[125] In a further letter from Joshua
Clarke to McMullan, he confirmed that 'I have now got my son
to hand over his drawings to me … He has also undertaken to

supervise the selection of the glass and carrying out of the work generally. Although I think that he has been magnificent over this as he loses all and gains nothing'.[126] The patrons decided to have Harry's design used on the window rather than that of his father. Harry, who was at this stage completely swamped with work, was still happy to ensure a successful outcome for both his father's firm and the client. He agreed to allow them to use his design and to remain in close contact with the process throughout its execution.

On 21 November 1918, a further letter from Joshua to McMullan showed that, unlike his son, he had no qualms about including a long inscription on the window 'the inscription will be in white letters with black background so it will be easily read from the floor and will not look so much of a patch as it looks at present'[127] This was a major bone of contention between Harry and the patrons. He had suggested, as an alternative, a small inscription on the window and a plaque to be placed underneath with as many details as required. Joshua was so keen to get this commission that he was not as worried about such details.

On 27 November 1918, Joshua wrote to McMullan 'as arranged, the work will be fixed within five months from this date … I note your remarks re design which I am sorry you wrote on, as front of design is not mine. However, I shall be able to place something over it to cover it up'.[128] The architect did not have as much respect for Harry's design as he should have had, as he appears to have scribbled over it. A final letter from Joshua to McMullan, on 3 December 1918, seems to have resolved this difficulty and confirmed that the window was made from a Harry Clarke design: 'I am at one with you that the matter is now settled. As regards my son handing me the design you are quite right in that, nevertheless, when the work is finished he will claim it back again'.[129]

From the correspondence referred to above, it is clear that the original design by Harry Clarke was used, with his permission, in the execution of this window and that he supervised the selection of the glass and the work in general. The Fr Thomas Dowling Memorial window, therefore, should be recognised in the canon of Harry Clarke's work and included as such in all references.[130] The window was initially conceived and designed by Harry Clarke and executed by the studio under his close supervision.

The Fr Thomas Dowling Memorial window is a two-light window (Fig. 40). A full-length figure of 'Christ – Prince of Peace' is depicted in the left-hand light. He is barefooted, showing the stigmata on his hands and feet and with birds at his feet. He is looking directly at the viewer and is wearing a rich ruby-red garment, edged with yellow. At the bottom of the window are two standing angels, facing to the left, who are praying over images of Cork and, to their right, blue demons are flying through a mist over the city. The steeple of St Anne's church, Shandon and St Mary's (North) Cathedral are clearly visible in a depiction of the city skyline. This image probably relates to the quotation 'the angels of peace shall weep bitterly' – Isaiah 33.9. There are also depictions of the four prophets, Elijah, Jeremiah, Zachariah and Micah, who foretold the coming of Christ – Prince of Peace, in colours of golden yellow. Two are at Christ's waist and two bookend the Cork City skyline at the bottom of the light. At Christ's head are depictions of St Fachtna on the right and St Gobnait on the left-hand side. Above the figure of Christ is Our Lady Enthroned, with St Francis de Sales and St Augustine. The overall colours of this light are of rich varied rubies, with a vivid blue and green background.

A full-length figure of 'St Francis of Assisi' is depicted on the right-hand light. He is also looking out at the viewer and is shown in the habit of his order, a robe of enhanced browns, ambers and yellows, on a background of blues. St Francis is holding a dove to his breast, a symbol of peace, and other birds are shown at his sandalled feet, and spill over into the left-hand light, to the feet of Christ. He is wearing a white cord and a large rosary around his waist. There are two

Fig. 40.
Fr Thomas Dowling
OSFC Memorial
Window,
Holy Trinity church,
Cork.
(Clodagh Evelyn
Kelly, Dublin)

saints at his head, two at his waist and two at the bottom of the light. These figures represent the prophets, apostles and advocates St David, St Basil, St Ambrose, St Gobnait of Ballyvourney, St Catherine and St Finbarr. At the top of the light is the figure of St Joseph, holding the infant Christ, with St Cecelia and St Teresa. Images of two standing angels praying for peace, in colours of rich pinks and ambers, are depicted at the base. They are facing to the right with demon heads threatening them from behind. This is probably a depiction of the devils of Jezebel destroyed by the prayers of angels. This light contains rich varied ambers and browns with a blue and green background.

A border of myrtle and olives, emblems of peace, runs completely around the window and into the tracery, thus tying the whole composition together. The inscription, over which there was so much controversy, is spread across both lights. It is depicted in white letters, with a few in yellow, on a black background. It reads:

> Memorial window erected by Cork Trades Unionists in grateful recognition of the services rendered by Very Rev. Thomas [Dowling] OSFC in ameliorating the lot of the workers during a period of unexampled distress caused by the European war 1914-1918. On behalf of Cork & District Trades & Labour Council – P. Lynch, President, T. Twomey, Secretary, the year of our Lord 1918.

Gordon Bowe stated that the final result 'is not unattractive, although the inscription is still too big and the painting and treatment of the glass lack his touch'.[131] Undoubtedly, the inscription is too big but this does not take too much from its overall impact. The window showcases Harry Clarke's trademark jewel-like colours and drawing details, such as the figures of Christ and St Francis who seem to be floating in space. The inclusion of the inscription in the window is the only record of the history of the Cork Council of Trade Unions for those years. In 2010, the fiftieth anniversary of the amalgamation of the two Cork Trade Councils was celebrated and [132] Mr Tom Bogue, a former chairperson who was also the historian for this celebration in 2010, confirmed that there is a gap in their records from 1916 to the 1940s. He also added that he was very glad the Cork Council of Trade Unions prevailed, rather than Harry Clarke, otherwise they would not have known about the window or its background, as there is no plaque below to indicate its history.

In spite of the controversy, the first window was very well received and admired and, as a result, a further two windows were commissioned from the Clarke Studio. On 21 December 1926, James O'Donovan and his wife[133] donated £700 to Fr Martin Hyland OFM Cap., Guardian of Holy Trinity Friary. Their request to erect two stained-glass windows was left completely in his hands. One was to be of the 'Sacred Heart' and the other of the 'Immaculate Conception'.[134] The first was to commemorate Mrs O'Donovan's parents, Mr and Mrs Robert Considine, and the second her husband's memory, when deceased. They asked for two slabs to be erected underneath the windows to this effect.[135]

By this time, Joshua Clarke had died and the business was being run by his two sons – Walter who looked after the church decorating and furnishing business side and Harry who dealt with the stained-glass side of the studio. On 12 January 1927, Walter Clarke wrote to Fr Laurence Dowling OFM Cap. to thank him for the commission to make two stained-glass windows.[136] Coincidently, the same architect, McMullan, was again employed on this project by Holy Trinity Friary.

Again, difficulties seem to have arisen, as contained in a letter from Walter to Fr Laurence on 19 January 1927: 'I have had a letter this morning from Mr McMullan with regards to the two stained-glass windows in which he asks us to submit designs and estimates. Having already sent the proposal of costs to you, we are at a loss quite to know what to do'.[137] Fr Laurence also seems to have had some concerns about the studio's experience of dealing with McMullan in the past, as detailed in a reply from Walter to him on 28 January 1927:

> I note your remarks about Mr McMullan and would say we have the most pleasant recollections of the assistance he gave during the progress of the Rev Fr Thomas window.

He did wish to help us out of our difficulties which often arise out of such important commissions.[138]

In a letter of 4 February 1927, Walter informed McMullan that 'my brother [Harry] proposes to come to Cork next Friday 11th inst. to inspect the position for the two stained glass windows in the Franciscan church'.[139] On 10 February 1927, Harry wrote to McMullan enclosing a diagram, showing measurements and templates for the two windows.[140]

On 23 March 1927, Harry wrote to McMullan 'we have therefore supplemented original idea with Munster saints, thus making the subject The Adoration of the Sacred Heart and The Adoration of the Immaculate Conception'.[141] Harry had decided to embellish the original idea, as single figures would not have adequately filled the spaces. On 7 March 1928, Walter Clarke wrote to Fr Laurence, enclosing a description of the three windows, and confirmed that they had been designed and made in the studio of J. Clarke & Sons, North Frederick Street, Dublin under the supervision of Harry Clarke RHA.[142]

On 21 December 1928, Harry wrote to McMullan:

As you know, they are very large and need very specialist attention. We hope to have them finished in the third week in January and may we add that they are a very complete window. We would say perhaps the best windows we have turned out yet in our Studios.[143]

A letter from Harry to John Sisk (the builder) on 19 January 1929, instructed that 'in case there shall be any doubt, we write to say that the two windows we are erecting in the Franciscan church in Cork are to be erected, one on either side of our window already there, in right transept'[144] This indicates Harry's in-depth knowledge of the earlier Fr Thomas Dowling Memorial Window and his intention to site the two new windows, in a triptych formation, to complement the earlier window.

A further problem arose in relation to the accuracy of the measurements for these two windows. In a letter to a Mr H. Dunne, one of his workers in Cork, Harry wrote 'we are rather surprised to note that the windows are not a fit as templates were taken by m/s Sisk who have heretofore always been deadly accurate in such work'.[145] Luckily the issue was resolved and a final letter was sent by Harry to Fr Laurence, on 15 February 1929, enclosing a statement.[146] This was to 'design supply and fit one two-light stained glass window, Sacred Heart @ £325 as well as 6' vent in base of each opening £14'[147] and 'design supply and fit one stained-glass window, Immaculate Conception @ £325'.[148]

The above correspondence demonstrates the extraordinary involvement of Harry Clarke, a stained-glass artist, in the minutiae of the business. It also highlights the difficulties that can arise, and that can be repeated, when conducting such a business.

The original pencil drawings, for the two O'Donovan Memorial windows, have been found in the Manuscript Library of Trinity College Dublin (TCD). They show drawings for 'The Adoration of the Sacred Heart'[149] (Fig. 41) and 'The Adoration of the Immaculate Conception'[150] (Fig. 42). Both are attributed in pencil to Philip Deegan whose work is very much in the Harry Clarke style.[151] Intriguingly, the drawing for the Virgin[152] is missing from the latter and instead it is in a separate drawing but without an attribution (Fig. 43). It is unclear if this is a standard drawing that was re-used or whether it was designed by another artist, or by Harry Clarke himself. Either way, all three drawings, are very much in Harry Clarke's style who, as his brother Walter confirmed, 'designs and supervises the production of all our windows'.[153]

The first O'Donovan window depicts 'The Adoration of the Sacred Heart' (Fig. 44). The left-hand light depicts Christ, in a vibrant ruby-red robe, which has a deep purple lining. He has a red cross in his halo and is pointing to his heart. He is barefooted and is showing the stigmata on his hands and feet. He is looking at the kneeling figure of St Gobnait of Ballyvourney. She is in the lower portion of the light and is looking up at Christ. Her robe is richly decorated in bright patterns of mixed vivid greens, interspersed with purple. She has a deep blue halo with a light grey rim. St Gobnait is

known as the 'patroness of bees' and she has a staff in one hand and a beehive in the other. A swarm of bees are ascending in a cloud from the hive and beyond the feet of Christ. These two elongated figures, in vivid contrasts of red and green, stand out against the background of blue. There are three angels on top of the light, in mauve and purple robes, facing the viewer.

The right-hand light depicts three saints of Munster. At the base is St Albert of Emly who is praying and holding a church and a rosary in his hands. The colours of his garment are in varied greens and

Left to right:
Fig. 41. Drawing for 'The Adoration of the Sacred Heart'.
Fig. 42. Drawing for 'The Immaculate Conception'.
Fig. 43. Drawing for 'Virgin – Immaculate Conception'.
(TCD M/s Library, Dublin)

ambers, which is also richly ornamented and reminiscent of an oriental carpet. He has a red halo with a light rim. Above him is St Ita, who is looking at the figure of Christ. She is holding three jewels, representing the three virtues or the monastic vows of Poverty, Chastity and Obedience. The colours of her robe are in warm neutral tones of mauve and purple. She is wearing a cloche-style hat and has a blue halo with a light rim. St Ita is known as the 'Brigid of Munster'. The figure at the top is St Finbarr, the patron saint of Cork City, who is also looking at Christ. He is holding a crozier, as well as a replica of the church he founded, in his light green-gloved hands. The colours of his robe are richly ornamented in deep blues and greens. He is wearing a crown and has a golden halo with a light rim. There are three angels at the top of the light, one of whom is facing the viewer, the other two are facing Christ, and all have purple wings.

The background to these two lights is a rich varied blue, with flowers, shells and star-like motif decorations. The overall background is in a patchwork or brick-like format and these contain Celtic swirls and motifs. There is a quatrefoil of two angel heads at the top of the window, with a depiction of the Holy Ghost above.

The second O'Donovan window depicts 'The Adoration of the Immaculate Conception' (Fig. 42). The left-hand light depicts the Virgin in a brilliant but delicate turquoise and deep blue robe, with elaborate gold braiding ornamentation. Her halo is blue with white dots that are reminiscent of a medieval custom, representing the stars. She is standing on a mauve crescent moon, a red serpent and a black globe. At her right-hand side is a flock of birds. She is looking at the bowed and kneeling figure below and seems to be stretching out her hands to embrace the whole world. The figure below her is St Munchin of Limerick. He is holding a burning flame-red torch in his pink-gloved hands. His robe is a mixture of rich purples with a wide green and blue ornamental border. He is wearing a crown and has a golden halo with a light rim.

Fig. 44.
'The Adoration of
the Sacred Heart',
stained-glass
window Holy Trinity
church, Cork.
(Clodagh Evelyn
Kelly, Dublin)

His appearance and dress have an oriental influence. On either side of the Virgin are two angels, with folded arms. They have grey and mauve wings and are facing the viewer. Their robes, in yellow and purple, are richly ornamented and they have purple halos. Above them are two angel heads with purple and ruby wings.

The right-hand light of the second O'Donovan window depicts the figures of three further Munster saints, all of whom are looking at the Virgin. The figure at the top is St Colman of Cobh. He is holding a cross in his light green-gloved hands. The colours of his robe are in varied greens with gold. He is wearing a hood and has a richly decorated golden halo. The figure beneath is St Fachtna of Rosscarbery, who is holding a staff in one hand and a purple book in the other. The colours of his robe are blue and turquoise, with a deep orange at his sleeves. He is wearing a crown and has a purple halo with a light rim. The bottom figure is St Brendan of Clonfert who is also known as 'The Navigator'. He is holding an oar in one hand and a small boat in the other. The colours of his robe are a rich ruby-red with a checkered orange and purple cape. He has a green halo with a light green rim. A flock of birds rise and fly higher, past St Brendan, and spill over into the right-hand light. There are two full-length angels, in blue robes with purple wings, at the top of the light. One is facing the viewer and one is facing the Virgin. Above them are two angel heads.

All of the figures are on a neutral grey and mauve background with decorations of flowers, shells and star-like motifs. The overall background, like the first O'Donovan Memorial window, is also a patchwork or brick-like format and these are embellished with Celtic swirls and motifs. In the trefoil, at the top of the window, are two angel heads with yellow halos and the Holy Ghost is depicted above.

A note in the Capuchin Friary in Cork says that two plaques were to have been fixed below each window in honour of the patrons. One was to read 'For the honour of God and in memory of Robert Considine (Senior) and his wife Catherine Roche Considine RIP' and the second to read, 'In honour of God and in memory of James O'Donovan and his wife Mary Catherine O'Donovan RIP'. These plaques have been lost during the repositioning of the windows from the sanctuary to their current position in the eastern nave.

Fig. 45.
'The Adoration of the Immaculate Conception', stained-glass window, Holy Trinity church, Cork.
(Clodagh Evelyn Kelly, Dublin)

These three very large and truly magnificent windows form an impressive triptych on the eastern nave of the church. John Ruskin said that 'the true perfection of a painted window is to be serene, intense, brilliant like jewellery, full of easily legible and quaint subjects and exquisitely subtle yet simple in its harmonies'.[154] All three of these Harry Clarke windows capture this jewel-like brilliance and subtlety through the use of vibrant colours, in particular the brilliant blues, purples and reds. These rich colours were probably influenced by Clarke's visit to Chartres Cathedral in 1914.[155] The bejewelled and richly decorated garments, all done in minute detail in each window, could have been influenced by the *Book of Kells*. This illuminated manuscript gospel book in Latin, created around AD 800, is richly decorated in lavish Celtic motifs. The manuscript is on permanent display at Trinity College Dublin.

The three windows in Holy Trinity church also incorporate an ethereal quality, which is one of the attractions of the compositions, particularly the figure of St Brigid who seems to float in the company of the saints of Munster. Gordon Bowe argued that Harry Clarke 'had evolved an idealised androgynous archetype, heavy-lidded, aesthetic, lost in reverie, a deathly pallor, red-gold hair and tapering fingers contrasting with deliberately stylised apparel'.[156] These archetype figures, usually depicted as more youthful looking than one might expect, are also featured in the windows. In particular, the face of the Virgin is very fetching and mysterious. It is reminiscent of the Virgin in 'The Annunciation', in St Joseph's church in Terenure Dublin[157] and her pose is similar to a design used for the 'St Doulough' window, in the Oblate Fathers Chapel, Raheny, Dublin.[158] The Virgin's robe is very stylised and bejewelled and this attention to detail is seen in all of the garments portrayed in these three windows.

Harry Clarke also manages to combine the beautiful with the macabre, as shown in the Fr Thomas Dowling Memorial window (Fig. 46). Here he depicts angels, surrounded by devils, weeping over the Cork City skyline. Harry would have been familiar with the 1913 Lockout in Dublin, which was a major industrial dispute about workers' rights to unionise and probably the greatest industrial dispute in Irish labour history. The trouble and grief caused by the antagonism between workers and employers, would have been seen by Harry in Dublin during the 1913 Lockout and this is probably reflected in this Cork window. The theme of peace and peace motifs in the window also echo the arbitration work between employers and trade unions, carried out by Fr Dowling during the same period in Cork.

The depiction of the Cork skyline in the window is reminiscent of a skyline in the 'St Louis IX, King of France and St Martin de Tours window', in Castletownsend church, County Cork.[159] The figure of St Gobnait, shown in a side-face profile, is mindful of Clarke's depiction of her in the Honan Chapel at UCC, including her trademark bees which are in both windows.

One of the best comments on Harry Clarke's work is encapsulated by E. Rankin, the noted Benedictine authority on ecclesiastical art.[160] He is quoted in a Clarke Studio invitation which said that 'the Clarke stained glass windows imitate nothing, not even the most beautiful works of the past. Everything is of the new, a work of freedom, of tasteful originality and of religious poetry'.

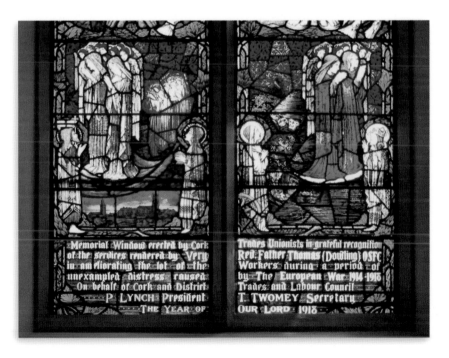

Fig. 46. Detail of the Fr Thomas Dowling OSFC Memorial Window,
Holy Trinity church, Cork. (Clodagh Evelyn Kelly, Dublin)

9

Additions and Alterations to Holy Trinity Church

By 1890, after a period of intermittent works over sixty-eight years, the Capuchin Order possessed a fine church and residence in Cork. This was not to be the end of the story of building at Holy Trinity church, however, as more additions and alterations were yet to come. The *Cork Examiner*, on 14 October 1905, reported on a proposal to build a memorial to Fr Bernard Jennings OSFC (1851-1905), who had set up many initiatives in the city to help young homeless and impoverished boys in the early 1900s. A committee was established which was led by the Lord Mayor and High Sheriff. It was decided unanimously that 'the scheme for the improvement of the sanctuary and altar, which Fr Bernard had contemplated, would be taken up by them and carried as the most fitting memorial to his memory'. The article went on to report that 'the probable cost of the work would be £3,000, the Community to contribute £2,000 and the rest to be fund-raised'. This extension was built upon property, which the Order was able to acquire, just behind the original church.

On 20 April 1908, the *Cork Examiner* reported that the design of the architectural firm of Ashlin & Coleman[161] was selected and John Delaney & Co. were contracted to erect this extension.

The overall supervising architect was again James F. McMullen. The article also stated that while the cost was brought down to £3,500, it did not include the 'expense of taking down, cleaning and repairing the O'Connell Memorial window and other contingent works'. Due to the nature of the site, and as had happened in the past, an extremely difficult and expensive portion of the work was in relation to the foundations which had to be laid at a depth of several feet underground. The article went on to describe:

> The ground space occupied by the new addition is 65 feet by 46 feet and 65 feet in height. This is divided into a sanctuary and two side chapels … The chapels are divided by arcades into tall, slender, clustered columns, with annulets, recessed bases and capitals, from which spring the arches supporting the richly panelled roofs. The chancel arch, separating the chancel from the nave, is supported by very ornate clustered columns, which give a fine bold finish to this portion of the sacred edifice and the ceiling of the sanctuary is similarly panelled to the other ceilings of the church.

This extension, however, has given the interior of the church an uneven look. The Assembly Rooms, which are directly behind the left-hand side of the northern gable wall, prevented the erection of a matching side chapel to the one on the right-hand side of the altar.

The next large-scale building project in the church was undertaken in the 1980s. The fabric of the building had deteriorated, due to a lack of maintenance and poor foundations. In addition, the liturgical revisions of the Second Vatican Council brought about a change in traditional Catholic observance and practice, including the conduct of Mass.[162] These considerations had also to be taken into account in this building project. Fr Eustace McSweeney OFM Cap., who was Guardian at the time, employed the architectural firm of Brian Wain and Associates to carry out this work. When the building was examined, however, they found such serious structural defects that demolishing the church and erecting a new one in its place was considered.

The problems with the building were first raised on 31 August 1979[163] and a lay fundraising committee was formed. On 28 November 1980,[164] the Minister General of the Capuchin Order asked that the alterations be 'in keeping with the mind of the church, with the demands of the present day liturgy and with the pastoral care of souls'. In January 1983, an article in *The Fold*, a liturgical magazine published by the Catholic Bishops of Cork, reported that Fr Eustace had said 'this is madness or an act of faith'. Fr Eustace went on to say in the article that:

> Some people might have advocated pulling down the old and building a new church. The founder of the Order, St Francis, rebuilt a church that had fallen into ruins. Rather than building a new one, therefore, that is what we are about to do – the same at Holy Trinity.

The church was closed and work began to tackle the restoration and liturgical redesign of the building. On 9 January 1982, the *Cork Examiner* reported that 'the costs will amount to £0.5m. Half the costs will come from the assets in the Capuchin Community and the other half from public subscriptions'. To underline the state of the building at the time, the article went on to describe:

> Dry rot in the roof, extreme woodworm damage on the side wall and severe dry rot also on the west wall. There

is no damp proofing under the floors. There is extensive water ingress under the surface of the walls with dry rot in the interior walls. All this damage will mean renewal and replacement. The spire has suffered severely from the ravages of the passing years and elaborate replacement of the flashing is imperative.

A fundraising campaign was launched in May 1882 and people were asked to give generously to help the restoration and redesign of Holy Trinity church. In any event, the church was renovated and reconstructed, in record time, and reopened within a year in 1982. The interior of the church, however, was completely altered in the process. The original Gothic furnishings, including the marble high altar and wooden confessionals, were removed. It is not clear if all of the interior alterations were necessary, but it was a controversial decision as many people bemoaned the demolition of the original interior of the church. Fr Eustace affirmed that the interior of the church was now in accordance with the edicts of the Second Vatican Council and was 'fully suitable for the celebration of liturgical services and for the active participation of the laity'.[165] This last major renovation work, however, did preserve the church building itself for future generations.

10

Interior of
Holy Trinity Church

Many refurbishment, alteration and redecoration schemes have been carried out in the interior of Holy Trinity church over the years. As a result, several plaques are displayed throughout the church marking such events. The following inscription, on the right-hand pillar of the main entrance to Holy Trinity church, reads: 'Memorial Church of Fr Theobald Mathew OSFC, Apostle of Temperance. Erected 1832. Sanctuary Extension Opened March 1908'.

On 6 November 1854, the *Cork Examiner* reported that a new organ had been installed in the church which was bought from the builder Mr John Seymour Murphy. Mrs James Halloran sang with a choir of thirty voices 'admirably calculated to show off the full power and rich tones of the instrument'. The organ cost £310[166] and, while there is still one in the balcony of the church today, it is unlikely to be the original organ.

In 1896, a special bell was baptised, replacing one that had been erected sixteen years earlier. Such a baptism is done with oil of chrism and is one of only three Sacraments, using this particular kind of oil, in Catholic services. These are Baptism, Holy Orders and Extreme Unction. The bell was donated by the O'Donovan family and named Mary, Patrick, Fr Francis.

The following inscription is in the sanctuary of the church, on the Fr Mathew Street side of the building, and reads:

> The foundation stone of the Fr Bernard Memorial was laid by the most Rev Dr O'Callaghan, Lord Bishop of Cork. (Rev Fr Fiacra [Brophy], Guardian) November 18th 1906. John Delaney & Co. Contractors, James F. McMullan CEMRIB Architect, Messrs Ashlin & Coleman, Architects.

On 20 April 1908, the *Cork Examiner* reported on the interior furnishings of the church, including the pulpit, which was executed by Messrs J.A. O'Connell & Son of Cork. It noted that the pulpit:

> Follows the usual polygonal style, the sides being very chastely carved. It is supported by a central pillar of red granite, surrounded by four more columns of white marble. The pulpit is ascended by marble stairs with massive burnished brass rails. In design and execution it is in keeping with the splendid church in which it is placed.

The article went on to describe the interior of the church as having 'rich floriated mosaic on the sanctuary floors and praedellas of the three altars, bordered by Sicilian marble steps'. The latter were executed by J.C. Edwards of Bandon. The communion rail, dividing the sanctuary from the nave and aisles, is composed of a 'Sicilian marble table supported by an arcade resting on coloured marble columns, on a Sicilian marble base, which rests on the kneeler of similar material'. This was executed by the sculptor, J.F. Davis, of Cork. The article also described the 'magnificent brass gates in front of the sanctuary and the gas brackets throughout'. These were executed by Messrs T.&C. McGloughlin of Dublin.

Fig. 47. The former Gothic high altar and sanctuary area, Holy Trinity church, Cork, *c.* 1940.
(Irish Capuchin Provincial Archives, Dublin)

From photographs in the Irish Capuchin Provincial Archives, one can see that the church originally had a large ornate Gothic-style high altar (Fig. 47) and the two side altars at the right-hand side were also made of marble. The rear wall, behind the altar, was decorated with painted images. In addition, a large ornate marble pulpit stood out prominently at the edge of the sanctuary, on the west side of the altar. Large wooden Gothic-style free-standing confessionals were also on the west side of the church.

As a result of the refurbishment works in the 1980s, the interior of the church is unrecognisable today. The marble high altar, pulpit and railings are gone. A new wooden sanctuary altar has been sited in the body of the church, on what was once the end of the original church building, and a small Blessed Sacrament Chapel installed on the right-hand side of the altar. The shrines to

Our Lady, St Francis and St Anthony have been retained but relocated around the church. The large free-standing wooden Gothic confessionals have been removed from the body of the church and replaced by recessed ones. The former were affectionately known as 'horse boxes'. The thick wooden casings that covered the cast-iron columns were removed and subsequently recovered in narrower wooden casings, to provide a better view of the altar.

The interior of the church itself is designed in a hall format, culminating in a flat north-facing altar wall. The church is lit on either side by seven large pointed windows, which have dulled glass of blue and yellow. Three of these, on the east wall of the church, are the Harry Clarke stained-glass windows, which are described in Chapter 8. The body of the church is divided on each side into nave and aisles by seven cast-iron columns. There is a wooden arch on the top of each column, crossing the nave. Each side arch has wooden arches with trefoil decorations in different designs.

The roof is also panelled in wood. On 25 November 1849, the *Cork Examiner* reported that 'as regards its internal finish and decoration, the splendid open work timber roof, which is somewhat like that of the Examination Hall in the Queen's College [now known as University College Cork (UCC)] is finished, together with the notable arches that span the roof'. It went on to state that the ceiling 'will be entirely composed of wood, appropriately ornamented, and after the designs of the splendid Catholic churches recently built in several parts of England by Mr Pugin'. It is interesting to note that, while the ceiling of the sanctuary was originally matched to the ornately panelled ceiling in the main body of the church, the latter is no longer decorated in this way (Fig. 48). This is probably due to the major refurbishment work carried out in the 1980s.

One can still see the large exterior stone pillars of the original church on either side of the sanctuary. The latter contains three

Fig. 48. The roof of the sanctuary and nave, Holy Trinity church, Cork, 2013.
(Clodagh Evelyn Kelly, Dublin)

arches with three painted cast-iron columns in the right-hand side altar. The recessed confessionals, on the western side of the church are accessed by the friars through the sacristy door, which also leads into the friary. This area also incorporates two large exterior stone pillars, which have been built into the fabric of the friary. There is a small gallery, high on the western side of the church, where friars who are ill can observe religious services. There is a balcony, containing an organ, running the full length of the south wall, which has three very large stained-glass windows.

In 2013, the porch was extended into the church to incorporate the entire area beneath the balcony. This area is now used to illustrate the history of the building of the church and its patron, Fr Theobald Mathew.

There are a number of plaques at the back of the church. One acknowledges the organ reconstruction in 1948 and commemorates Fr Dominic O'Connor OFM Cap., Brigade Chaplain IRA (1916-21). Another commemorates the 150th anniversary of the inauguration of Fr Mathew's Temperance Campaign, on 8 December 1988.

Currently, there is a restored rare wooden reredos altar located at the back of the sanctuary (Fig. 49). This was carved over a hundred years ago by Ferdinand Stuflesser of Ortisei, in Italy. The company was founded in 1875 and is still in existence today.[167] This altar is sited directly under the O'Connell Memorial window which dwarfs it somewhat. It was donated by Bridget Rochfort in memory of her mother. It was originally installed in St Francis'

Fig. 49. The reredos altar by Ferdinand Stuflesser (1855-1926) of Ortiesi, Italy, Holy Trinity church, Cork. (Clodagh Evelyn Kelly, Dublin)

chapel in Rochestown, County Cork where the Capuchin Order has a friary, church and school. The reredos altar has three poly-chrome images depicting 'The Last Supper' (under the altar table), 'The Presentation in the Temple' (on the left-hand side) and 'The Teaching in the Temple' (on the right-hand side).

In the early 1990s, Fr Dermot Lynch OFM Cap. commissioned a special wooden oak carved altar and pulpit for the church. They were designed by Ben Russell, an English artist living and working in Kealkil, Bantry, County Cork. They are placed in the body of the church at the edge of the sanctuary area. Emblems from the Passion of Christ are carved throughout the pieces, echoing similar emblems on the reredos altar, as well as an image of the Lamb of God on the altar table. The latter gives a nod to the early Flemish fifteenth-century Ghent Altarpiece by Hubert (1370-1476) and Jan Van Eyck (c1395-1441) depicting the 'Adoration of the Mystic Lamb'. Also depicted are the coat of arms of the Capuchin Order (on the pulpit), and prayer of St Francis (on the altar). The entire sanctuary area and steps are now carpeted in red. What one can see in the church today is a relatively plain and unattractive interior whose artistic merit is preserved by some magnificent stained-glass windows (Fig. 50).

11

The Capuchins in Irish Civil and Cultural Life

In the years before the Easter Rising in 1916, the Irish language, literature, history and sport were being revived, or re-invented, in the quest for a national identity or an Irish Ireland. This has become known as the Gaelic Revival.

In 1885, the Gaelic Athletic Association (GAA) was founded by Michael Cusack (1847-1906), a teacher from County Clare. The aim of the GAA was to replace English games, such as soccer, cricket and tennis, with Gaelic football, hurling and handball. During the cultural revival of the 1880s, Archbishop Thomas Croke (1824-1902) recognised the potential for national games to replace the apathy and drunkenness that existed among many Irish people. As a result, the GAA was strongly supported by Catholic clergy and Irish nationalists.

In 1893, due to concerns about the decline of the Irish language, *Conradh na Gaeilge*, also known as the Gaelic League, was founded by, among others, Eoin MacNeill (1869-1945), the Irish scholar and nationalist who convened its first meeting, and Douglas Hyde (1860-1949) who became its first president. Hyde, who was born in Castlerea, County Roscommon was a noted Irish scholar and subsequently became the first President of Ireland (1938-45).

The Gaelic League reinvigorated interest in the Irish language and in native customs and culture. It also provided a cultural transformation, giving the Irish language a respect and status that it had lacked. In addition, it promoted Irish music, dancing and singing, as well as literary competitions and festivals. This movement was part of an aspiration to bring about an independent Ireland, which the Irish poet and nationalist Pádraig Pearse (1879-1916) described as 'not free merely but Gaelic as well'.

Before Ireland became an independent Republic, the official culture was, by and large, geared towards making Irish people good citizens of the British Empire. Some religious orders who were involved in education, pursued a certain kind of respectability which espoused English standards and English values. With the advent of the nationalist movement, they found themselves wrong-footed and had to hastily introduce Gaelic games and other elements into their curriculum, as well as articles in Irish into their journals[168]. The Capuchin Order in general, however, seems to have always supported Irish cultural and civil activities and has made an immeasurable contribution to Irish public life over the years.

Fr Edwin Fitzgibbon OFM Cap. (1874-1938), who lived in Cork for most of his life, played a leading role in third-level education and in the promotion of Gaelic games. Born in Ballynona, County Cork, into a large Irish-speaking farming family, he was an avid sportsman. However, he gave up sport for religion and entered the Capuchin Order where he studied philosophy at Louvain University in Belgium. He was subsequently appointed Professor of Philosophy (1911-36) at University College, Cork (UCC) and was one of the first staff members of the newly formed National University of Ireland (NUI).[169] He had a life-long interest in hurling and the Fitzgibbon Cup, which he personally funded, is still the premier hurling championship trophy among higher education institutes in Ireland. The cup was made by the Cork silversmiths, William Egan & Sons, who were formerly located in Patrick Street. A photograph shows Fr Fitzgibbon, presenting the Fitzgibbon Cup (Fig. 51) to Richard Molloy, captain of the UCC Hurling Team who defeated University College Dublin (UCD) (8-1 to 7-4) in the final of the inter-colleges hurling competition, held in Dublin in 1928. Professor P.J. Merriman, Provost of UCC, is standing beside the UCD captain. Fr Fitzgibbon is buried in the Capuchin Cemetery at Rochestown, County Cork. A fellow Capuchin Friar, Fr Cyril O'Sullivan OFM Cap. (1887-1921), who also had a PhD from Louvain University, joined Fr Fitzgibbon on the teaching staff. Both were instrumental in establishing the Philosophy Department at UCC and built up the reputation of this Department in the College.

Fig. 51. Presentation by Fr Edwin Fitzgibbon OFM Cap.,
of the Fitzgibbon Cup, to the Captain of the UCC Hurling Team, 1928.
(Irish Capuchin Provincial Archives, Dublin)

Interest in the promotion of the Irish language and culture was also a feature in the lives of some other Capuchins. Fr Aloysius Travers OFM Cap. (1870-1957), a native of Cork City, joined the Capuchin Order in 1887 and was ordained a priest in 1894. During his time as President of Fr Mathew Hall, Church Street, Dublin, he founded *Feis Maitiu*, along with Fr Arthur Darby. This was to encourage such pursuits as performance art, drama and verse-speaking. It is the longest-running festival in Ireland. In 1927, Fr Michael O'Shea OFM Cap. founded *Feis Maitiu* in Cork which influenced the growth of similar cultural events through-out Munster. He was universally known as *an t-Athair Micheal*. He was also a promoter of the Irish language and one of the first in Cork to wear the *Fainne*, which is a pin used to identify an Irish speaker. Both *Feiseanna* are still running today and have become major features in the cultural landscape of Ireland as well as a launch pad for the careers of many singers and actors. While the Capuchin Order no longer has a role in the organisation of the *Feiseanna*, it continues to support its goals.

Fr Augustine Hayden OFM Cap. (1870-1954) also had a strong interest in the Gaelic Revival and, in particular, in preserving the Irish language. He was well known for the missions he conducted in *Gaeltacht* areas. In 1904, along with Shan O'Cuiv, he estab-lished the Irish Language College at Ballingeary, County Cork, which was the first college of its kind in the country.

Members of the Capuchin Order have made a major contribu-tion to Irish educational institutions, particularly at UCC. As noted above, Fr Edwin Fitzgibbon was one of the first members of staff at UCC and he was succeeded as Professor of Philosophy by Fr James O'Mahony OFM Cap. (1897-1962). Fr James, assisted by Fr Kieran O'Callaghan OFM Cap. (1894-1967), worked at UCC for many years, and wrote several influential books on the topics of philosophy and theology. He had the distinction, unique up to then, of obtaining the *Agrege* in Philosophy from Louvain University. Fr James held the post of professor and was also Vice-President of UCC. He was closely associated with the launching of the Mercier Press in Cork, by Sean Feehan, which published many of his best-selling books. It is interesting to note that the first book published by the Mercier Press, in 1944, was *The Music of Life* by Fr James O'Mahony OFM Cap. Other notable Capuchin academics at UCC were Professor Peter Dempsey OFM Cap. (1914-2004), who held the Chair of Psychology and helped found what is known today as the Irish Management Institute, and Fr Pascal Larkin OFM Cap. (1894-1976), who lectured in economics and wrote several influential books.

The *Capuchin Annual* was published for forty-seven years, between 1930 and 1977, by the Capuchin Order in Ireland. Its motto was '*do Chum gloire de agus onora na hEireann*' (for the glory of God and the honour of Ireland). Its ethos was the promotion of, and education in, Christian values and a Catholic way of life. It had many unique ways of exploring these subjects, including a high level of contributors. Its first editor was Fr Senan Moynihan OFM Cap. (1900-70) and he was succeeded by Fr Henry Anglim OFM Cap. (1910-77). From the beginning, the *Capuchin Annual* maintained a high standard with articles from leading educators, politicians and writers of the period, such as Thomas MacGreevy, Michael Bowles, Ben Kiely, Francis MacManus and Augustine Martin who were regular contributors. MacGreevy, who was Director of the National Gallery of Ireland (1950-63), wrote many articles for the *Capuchin Annual* that explored the life and work of Irish artists.[170]

The distinctive cover of the *Capuchin Annual* depicted *St Francis and the Wolf* (Fig. 52). It had a brown cover and the writing was depicted in orange with a splash of green for grass and orange for a sunset and the saint's halo. This was designed

by the Irish artist Sean O'Sullivan RHA (1906-64) who also contributed other drawings to the *Capuchin Annual* over the years.
The *Capuchin Annual* was an influential social and cultural publication that discussed religious, historical and literary topics of
the day. Its articles concentrated on Irish interests in a variety of
subjects, from both at home and abroad, including philosophy, literature, art, poetry and nationalism and they were well illustrated
with cartoons, drawings and photographs. The *Capuchin Annual*
was an Irish institution for many years and had a readership of
25,000 in its heyday. Patrick Kavanagh (1904-67), the well-known
Irish poet, described it as 'an amazing phenomenon of modern
political Catholic Ireland'.[171] It championed Irish artists, such as
Harry Clarke, Sean O'Sullivan, Jack B. Yeats, John Lavery and
William Orpen. It also championed new Irish writers such as

Fig. 52.
The cover of the
Capuchin Annual by
Sean O'Sulllivan RHA
(1906-64). (Clodagh
Evelyn Kelly, Dublin)

Maurice Walsh and Pearse Hutchinson. Overall, the *Capuchin Annual* played a role in defining the culture of Ireland in the early turbulent decades of the newly independent country.

Some Capuchin Friars were also active in public life. For example, Fr Thomas Dowling OFM Cap. (1874-1950), who was born in Freshford, County Kilkenny. His early years were dedicated to the promotion of the total abstinence movement. He was subsequently attached to Holy Trinity church in Cork and was responsible for the Fr Mathew Pavilion at the Cork International Exhibition in 1902. Designed by the architect J.F. McMullen, it was a small building in a French neo-Classical style. It housed a selection of memorabilia and relics of Fr Mathew.[172] These included wooden models of Holy Trinity church, which is now in the Irish Architectural Archive in Dublin, and Thomastown Castle, where Fr Mathew was reared in County Tipperary. A commemorative fountain in honour of Fr Mathew was also installed at this exhibition. Executed by Henry Cutler, it is made of reinforced Portland cement, a new building material for the time. The upper tier, which was added later, is made of cast-iron. The fountain originally stood in front of the Industrial Hall, as part of the Cork International Exhibition in 1902, but it is now located in the ornamental pond in what has become known as Fitzgerald's Park, in the Mardyke, Cork.[173]

Fr Thomas had studied social reform and is probably best known for his work as an arbitrator between employers and trade unions. He founded the first Conciliation Board in Cork, with an equal number of employers and workers, and was its first chairman. This was also the first such organisation in an English-speaking country. His arbitration work, which was carried out during a period of unparalleled industrial unrest in the city, earned him the respect of both parties alike. This was also during the period of the First World War, when the economy of

Cork was in free-fall. Wages were failing to keep pace with rising prices, resulting in a 'seething cauldron' of demonstrations, labour disputes and strikes.

As chairman of the Conciliation Board, Fr Thomas presided over many trade disputes. One of the most notorious was a crucial wage dispute between the Tramway Workers and the Company, for which he brokered a successful settlement. In 1918, in recognition of the work he had carried out as an arbitrator and mediator, the Cork and District Trades and Labour Council donated a stained-glass window to Holy Trinity church, which is still in place today, and is described in Chapter 8. The window was unveiled by Dr Daniel Cohalan, Bishop of Cork (1915-52). On 8 May 1919, the *Cork Examiner* gave a very fulsome description of the proceedings. The ceremony was attended by representatives of both employers and trade unions. Prior to the ceremony, the Cork Workingman's Brass and Reed and the Connolly Memorial Fife and Drum Bands played a selection of music outside the church.

In his address, Dr Cohalan recalled that the first strike settled through the arbitration of Fr Thomas dated back to 10 December 1901. He paid tribute to Fr Thomas for bringing capital and labour together to establish a joint Conciliation Board in the city. He said that neither worker nor employer liked disputes, yet differences would arise. He went on to say that, in modern times, Pope Leo XIII (1810-1909) was a great advocate of a minimum wage and said that 'every worker is entitled to a minimum wage which will maintain him in frugal comfort and the employer that gives less is guilty of injustice'. While he insisted on a minimum wage, Pope Leo XIII also said that workers may look for better conditions. Dr Cohalan went on to urge the Conciliation Board not to confine its energy to disputes between the employer and the worker, but to also endeavour to get a grasp of all the great labour problems, such as housing and possible changes in the future.

In this context, it is interesting to note how long it took for such ideas to be implemented in the country. The statutory minimum wage only came into existence in Ireland following the introduction of the National Minimum Wage Act 2000. As well as that, successive National Wage Agreements in the 1980s-'90s between the Irish Government and the Social Partners, included other labour issues, such as programmes to help unemployed people.

On 5 May 1919, the *Cork Examiner* reported that the Cork and District Trades and Labour Council also held a commemorative dinner that evening, in the Victoria Hotel on Patrick Street, in honour of Fr Thomas. Once again the attendance was representative of trade and commerce in the city. It reported that it was a purely temperance dinner in recognition of Fr Thomas's brotherhood with the Apostle of Temperance, Fr Mathew. The Council commissioned an illuminated address[174] which they presented to Fr Thomas, as well as bestowing on him the additional title of Honorary President of the Council. The address stated:

> By unanimous resolution of the above Council it was decided that, on the occasion of the unveiling of the Memorial Window, erected to commemorate your work in the cause of labour, we should present to you in engrossed form the following minutes taken from the records of our Council Meeting held Thursday 17th September 1917. On the motion of Michael Egan T.C.J.I., seconded by Jeremiah Kelleher, Alderman, J.P., the following resolution was unanimously passed – 'that we, the delegates of the Cork & District Trades & Labour Council, representing organised labour in Cork and District, fully believe it is the unanimous opinion of thousands of workers we represent that the Very Reverend Father Thomas OSFC deserves any honour we can confer on him for the great

services he has rendered to the cause of labour'. We accordingly hereby confer on him the highest honour in our gift and declare him hereby elected Honorary President of Cork & District Trades & Labour Council. Patrick Lynch, President, Denis Kiely, Vice-President, J. O'Sullivan, Treasurer, Thos. Twomey, Secretary. In conveying above resolution to you Dear Father Thomas, permit me to state that your record since this unexampled honour was conferred to you has endeared you still more to the workers it is my privilege to represent and we greet you not merely as our Honorary President but as Chairman of Cork Conciliation Board which has established harmonious relations between capital and labour.

Politically, there was also unrest in the country at the time, due to the Conscription Act. This would have resulted in a compulsory call-up for Irish men of a certain age to fight for Britain in the First World War. It was a most unpopular move and even the Irish bishops became involved in the debate. On 18 April 1918, they directed the clergy to celebrate a public Mass of Intercession, in every church in Ireland 'to avert the scourge of conscription with which Ireland is now threatened'.[175] Fr Thomas was also in tune with the anti-Conscription mood and spoke out about it at rallies in Cork. On 24 April 1918, the *Cork Examiner* reported that 'Fr Thomas, President of the Cork United Trades, gave a great speech against conscription which evoked an extraordinary show of enthusiasm' and went on to say 'in agreement with the united labour of all Ireland, Cork labour assembled on the Grand Parade and unanimously adopted the resolution against the application of the Conscription Act' (Fig. 53).

On 21 June 1918, Fr Thomas was made a Freeman of Cork City. The honour was presented to him by the Lord Mayor,

Fig. 53. Fr Thomas Dowling OFM Cap., addressing an anti-conscription rally, Grand Parade, Cork, 1918. (Irish Capuchin Provincial Archives, Dublin)

Thomas C. Butterfield, and his citation noted that it was conferred 'in recognition of his splendid service to the city in his successful mediation in the frequent labour disputes since the start of the war'. In 1920, another tribute was paid to him when the Senate of the University of Ireland conferred an honorary degree. This was presented to Fr Thomas by Professor J.P. Merriman, President of UCC, and the citation for his degree of LL.D. read: 'By his tact, energy and good judgment, he has been the means of a much better feeling between employers and employed and has thus conferred a great benefit on the community generally'.

In 1926, while still Guardian of Holy Trinity Friary, Fr Thomas volunteered to go to the Capuchin Mission in California, United States of America, where he became a noted preacher and promoter of temperance. Before leaving Cork, he made a moving and telling address to the Cork District Council of Trade Unions where he outlined the basis for his arbitration work:

> It is not wealth but worth that counts. It is not riches, or power, or position that makes a man, but that the real test of manhood is service to all fellows. Your lot, the lot of every worker in the world, is to build up the fabric of society – to woo and win from the hoard of the secret treasures of the earth what makes for human progress. In your association together as trade unionists your watch-word is the enabling and uplifting of your fellow worker … The best interest of society is conserved, the highest social progress ensured and trade and commerce developed more assuredly in a community where a strong trade union movement exists; provided that movement is properly guided and is based on the only principles that ensure human advancement, namely Christian principles … Trade unionism is very generally misunderstood and that misunderstanding is sometimes not confined to those who imagine that it is antagonistic to their interests. Prejudice blinds those who see in it a social danger and leads those to exaggerate every mistake made by those within the movement who, failing to accurately interpret its principles, seem to be activated by blind antagonism to the entire existing social order. In forming these ideals, such people forget the limitations of human judgment and forget that, when men suffer under a grievance, they are inclined to centre all their efforts to remedy it and to lose sight of the consequences that may accrue from the methods they employ to effect this remedy…The workers of Cork know the principles of trade unionism and value them as the workers of few

other cities know or value them. For this Council has done more to win credit for the movement and to uplift those it represents than any similar body of which I have any knowledge.[176]

Fr Thomas died in Watts, California, in 1950, where he was a leading figure in the Capuchin Mission and well known as a public speaker, both as a preacher and a lecturer.

On 24 January 1951, Patrick O'Shea, Secretary of the Cork District Council, wrote a letter of sympathy to the Guardian of the Cork Friary on hearing of the death of Fr Thomas. O'Shea wrote that 'many of the older workers remember with pride their association with him and the great work he performed on their behalf in the days when mighty forces were ranged against organised labour in this country'. While he also made a success of his work in the Capuchin Mission in the United States of America, nevertheless, the mediation and arbitration work, carried out by Fr Thomas in Cork, was not forgotten and was also fully appreciated.

12

The Capuchins and Irish Nationalism

Irish nationalism evolved from a reaction against British imperialism and an attempt to revive Gaelic culture. Catholicism, as the predominant religion, played an important part in helping nationalism to become an effective mass movement. This association was recognised by Daniel O'Connell when he sought to join with Fr Mathew and his temperance movement. Initially, the Catholic bishops opposed violence as a means of promoting the nationalist cause. However, the growing support for the Sinn Féin party and the execution of the leaders of the 1916 Rising, who were subsequently seen as martyrs for the cause, resulted in Church leaders overlooking any theological arguments. This change was also probably linked to the historical British persecution of the Catholic Church in Ireland. This sense of unity helped to integrate Catholicism with nationalist identity.

The Irish hierarchy supported the mainly non-violent Irish Parliamentary Party in the 1880s and the campaign for Home Rule in 1886-1920. As it espoused violence, they did not support the Irish republican movement until 1921 and opposed the anti-Treaty side in the Civil War. In spite of this, many priests made up their own minds and supported the different sides of the Irish independence movement in their own way.

The trend towards violence in Ireland has also to be seen in the broader European context. At the time, the demands of political radicals and revolutionaries, suffragettes and unionised workers were all challenging the political and social order throughout the European Continent. As the well-known Irish poet, William Butler Yeats (1865-1939) said at the time 'a terrible beauty is born' and utter change lay ahead.

There are strong links between the Capuchin Order and the Irish nationalist movement, although this was probably due to an individual rather than an Order-wide approach. Some of the Capuchin Friars based in Church Street, Dublin were prominently associated with the independence movement and the leaders of the 1916 Rising. These included friars such as Fr Albert Bibby OFM Cap. (1877-1925), Fr Augustine Hayden and Fr Aloysius Travers.

Fr Albert Bibby was born in Bagenalstown, County Carlow. His family owned a woollen mill at Greensland as well as two drapery outlets in Kilkenny city. He was one of the first Capuchin Friars to receive a BA from the Royal University. He later became a Professor of Philosophy and Theology at UCC and Fr Dominic O'Connor OFM Cap. (1883-1933) was one of his first students. A photograph of the two priests, Fr Albert and his former pupil Fr Dominic, walking outside the church of St Mary of the Angels, Church Street, Dublin (Fig. 54) shows them conversing and their paths crossed many times during their activities with nationalists. Fr Albert ministered to a number of nationalist prisoners in Kilmainham Jail and was present at the execution of Sean Heuston (1897-1916). Heuston was Captain of Na Fianna Éireann and Leader of D Company, First Battalion Dublin Brigade. On 16 December 1920, Fr Albert was arrested, along with Fr Dominic, during a raid by British forces on the Capuchin Friary at Church Street, Dublin. Fr Albert was detained for several hours, in Dublin Castle, and subsequently released while Fr Dominic was sentenced to five years' penal servitude. When the Four Courts in Dublin was attacked on 27 June 1922, Fr Albert was present in the building, along with Fr Dominic. Both priests remained with the anti-Treaty volunteers until the Four Courts was evacuated. In June 1924, Fr Albert died in the United States of America where he had become pastor at Santa Inez in California.

Fr Augustine Hayden was born in Gowran, County Kilkenny. In 1884 he was one of the first pupils to be admitted to the newly opened Seraphic School, founded by the Capuchin Order, in Rochestown, County Cork. He was present at the surrender of Éamonn Ceannt (1881-1916) at the South Dublin Union and ministered to Ceannt before his execution. Ceannt was a member of the Military Council IRB, Director of Communications, Irish Volunteers and commandant of the Fourth Battalion,

Fig. 54. Fr Albert Bibby OFM Cap. and Fr Dominic O'Connor OFM Cap. (right) walking outside the church of St Mary of the Angels, Church Street, Dublin, 1921. (Irish Capuchin Provincial Archives, Dublin)

Fig. 55. Fr Augustine Hayden OFM Cap. at the marriage of Terence MacSwiney and Muriel Murphy at Bromyard, England, 1919. (Irish Capuchin Provincial Archives, Dublin)

Dublin Brigade. Fr Augustine ministered to Michael Mallin (1874-1916) before his execution, as well as Con Colbert (1888-1916). Mallin was a socialist and second in command of the Irish Citizens Army, under James Connolly (1870-1916). Connolly, one of the 1916 leaders, was a socialist, a labour leader and a journalist, as well as Commandant General of the Dublin Forces during the Rising. Colbert was one of the first members of Fianna Éireann and a captain in the Volunteers. Fr Augustine accompanied Fr Aloysius Travers to visit Pádraig Pearse and James Connolly. Pearse, one of the leaders of the 1916 Rising, was also a teacher, barrister and poet. Fr Augustine was instrumental in securing the surrender of Thomas MacDonagh (1878-1916) at Jacobs biscuit factory. MacDonagh, as well as being a political activist, was also a poet and a playwright.

In June 1917, Fr Augustine officiated at the marriage of Terence MacSwiney (1879-1920), Lord Mayor of Cork, to Muriel Murphy, in Bromyard in England (Fig. 55). She was a member of a well-known brewing/distilling family in Cork. He also officiated at the marriage of MacSwiney's daughter Maire to Ruairi Brugha in Cork in 1941. Ruairi was the son of Cathal Brugha (1874-1922) who was second in command to Éamonn Ceannt at the South Dublin Union and severely injured during its defence. He was elected President of the first Dail in 1918 and, having stepped aside in favour of Eamon de Valera (1882-1975), became Minister for Defence and Chairman of the Army Council. In spite of trying to prevent it, he was subsequently killed during the Civil War. De Valera was second in command to Thomas MacDonagh of the Dublin Brigade during the 1916 Rising. He opposed the Treaty and formed Fianna Fail in 1925 and served multiple terms as Taoiseach and President of the country. Fr Augustine died in Cork and is buried in Rochestown Cemetery where, coincidently, he had served as rector of Rochestown College (1896-1907).

Fr Aloysius Travers (Fig. 56), a native of Cork City, was born into a prominent and devotedly Catholic family. He was a major promoter of the temperance movement and was president of Fr Mathew Hall (1904-13). In 1908, he published the *Fr Mathew Record*, which he also used to promote a 'Buy Irish' campaign. Fr Aloysius was involved in ministering to the leaders of the 1916 Rising during their imprisonment. He was also instrumental in conveying messages between the volunteers and the British Army and advocated on behalf of the nationalist prisoners to try to secure fair and lenient treatment for them. In his capacity as a priest, he was only allowed to give Holy Communion but was not permitted to be present at the executions of Pádraig Pearse and Thomas MacDonagh. Following strenuous protests, priests were subsequently allowed to remain at later executions and Fr Aloysius was present at the execution of

Fig. 56.
Fr Aloysius Travers OFM Cap.
(1870-1957). (Irish Capuchin
Provincial Archives, Dublin)

James Connolly. He was also the person who had to inform the Pearse and MacDonagh families of the death of their sons. Margaret Pearse, brother of Pádraig Pearse, described that:

On Wednesday 3rd May, at about 10 o'clock a.m., the Rev Fr Aloysius arrived to break to us the terrible news that Pat had made the supreme sacrifice – that he had died that morning at a quarter to four. Fr Aloysius consoled, advised and strengthened us. He gave us details of the last hours, told us how bravely Pat, Tom Clarke and Thomas MacDonagh had died.[177]

Thomas Clarke (1858-1916) was arguably the key figure of the 1916 Rising. He was a proponent of armed resistance and spent fifteen years in prison prior to his involvement in the Rising. Subsequently, Fr Aloysius, along with Fr Albert Bibby, ministered to Willie Pearse (1881-1916) and they were with him at his execution. Willie was the young brother of Pádraig Pearse. It has been speculated that Fr Aloysius undertook a secret mission to Pope Benedict XV (1854-1922) in connection with the Irish struggle. He later championed the cause of various labour leaders in Dublin. Fr Aloysius is buried in Glasnevin Cemetery in Dublin.

During the period of the Easter Rising 1916, the Father Mathew Hall in Church Street, Dublin was handed over as a first-aid station to Edward (Ned) Daly (1891-1916).[178] Daly was Commandant of the Dublin First Battalion and the youngest to be executed in the aftermath of the Rising. There is a portrait of him in the Irish Capuchin Provincial Archives (Fig. 57) by the well-known Irish artist Sean O'Sullivan that is one of a number of portraits he painted of the 1916 leaders.

On 23 April 1917, Nannie O'Reilly, wife of 'The O'Rahilly', wrote to Fr Albert Bibby to express her regret that a Mass in honour of the rebels of 1916 could not be held in the Church Street Friary, 'as you did so much for the men who died'. She added, 'thank God we had the Mass at Mount Argus[179] ... as you say, the spirit was splendid, without any outward demonstration ... so that the priests who refused us might easily have had more courage'.[180] Michael Joseph O'Rahilly (1875-1916) who was known as The O'Rahilly, was a founder member of the Irish Volunteers. In spite of his

Fig. 57.
'Portrait of Edward
(Ned) Daly' by Sean
O'Sullivan RHA (1906-64).
(Irish Capuchin Archives
Artwork Collection, Dublin)

Fig. 58.
Fr Dominic O'Connor
OFM Cap. in British Army
chaplain's uniform, *c.* 1916.
(Irish Capuchin Provincial
Archives, Dublin)

misgiving about the 1916 Rising, The O'Rahilly joined in and is reputed to have said, 'I have helped to wind up the clock, I might as well hear it strike'. He died of gunshot wounds while escaping from the General Post Office (GPO), which was the central location of the Easter Rising in Dublin in 1916.

Members of the Holy Trinity Friary were also involved in the Independence movement. For example, Fr Dominic O'Connor OFM Cap., who was born in County Cork. His father was a teacher, whose household was devotedly Catholic, and several of his siblings joined religious congregations. He volunteered for chaplaincy work during the First World War, spending about two years with the British Forces (Fig. 58). Considering his later activities, it is interesting to note how he described his reasons for volunteering for the British Army in a letter to his sister, who was a nun (Sister Considine). It was written around 1916-17 from the 21 Station Hospital, Salonika Forces, Macedonia:

Well someone had to do the work and, when those who had done all the recruiting were too cowardly to go, there was nothing left except to have us who were anti-recruiters to go and help the souls of the soldiers that they had sent out.[181]

Fr Dominic resigned his post in the British Army in 1917 and returned to the Holy Trinity Friary in Cork. He became active in nationalist circles and was appointed chaplain to the Cork Brigade of IRA volunteers by Tomás MacCurtain (1884-1920) who was Lord Mayor of Cork from 30 January to 20 March 1920. This was a controversial appointment, as detailed in a letter of

Fig. 59.
Statue of Tomás
MacCurtain (1884-1920),
Lord Mayor of Cork
30 January-
20 March 1920 by
Domhnall O'Murchadha
(1914-91) sited outside
Cork City Hall.
(Clodagh Evelyn
Kelly, Dublin)

22 February 1922, from the Bishop of Cork, Dr Daniel Cohalan, to Fr Edwin Fitzgibbon 'now I put it to you that a lay body has no authority to confer an ecclesiastical honour from a lay authority'.[182] MacCurtain (Fig. 59) was connected first with the Blackpool branch of the Gaelic League and subsequently became Lord Mayor of Cork. He was commandant of the IRA in Cork and was murdered by British Forces at his home in the city. Fr Dominic was the first to appear at MacCurtain's home in Blackpool on the morning that the Sinn Féin Lord Mayor was murdered.

On Good Friday 1916, James Ryan (1891-1970) travelled by train to Cork to deliver instructions from Sean MacDermott (1885-1916) to MacCurtain. Ryan was a founder member of the Irish Volunteers and a medical doctor in the GPO during the 1916 Rising and subsequently a Minister in several Fianna Fail governments. MacDermott was a political activist and a writer and one of the leaders of the 1916 Rising. On his return to Dublin, Ryan was ordered by Eoin MacNeill (1867-1945) to go to Cork again, this time by motor car, to deliver another dispatch. These orders, cancelling the fateful Easter Sunday manoeuvres, were to be given to Pierce McCann in Tipperary, to MacCurtain in Cork and to the Officer in Command in Tralee.[183] MacNeill was an Irish scholar and nationalist who co-founded the Gaelic League and became chief of staff of the Irish Volunteers. However, he disagreed with the planned 1916 Rising and so countermanded the orders from Pádraig Pearse. This resulted in the general confinement of the Rising to the Dublin area.

Fr Dominic also served MacCurtain's friend and successor as Lord Mayor, Terence MacSwiney (1879-1920), who was also the officer commanding the First Cork Brigade. In March 1920, MacSwiney said in his acceptance speech as Lord Mayor of Cork that the 'circumstances of the vacancy in the office of Lord Mayor inevitably garnered the filling of it and I come here more as a soldier stepping into the breach than an administrator to fill the post in the municipality'.[184] He was Lord Mayor of Cork from 20 March to 20 October 1920. MacSwiney was subsequently arrested under the Defences of the Realm Act. Fr Dominic recorded that MacSwiney had told him that he was arrested on 12 August 1920 at 7.40 p.m. without warrant, without any charges whatsoever against him, and that an attempt to frame a charge was later made. This was done when a second raid was made that night, at 11.30 p.m., during curfew hours. During the second raid, many documents were taken from his personal desk and other documents were 'found' which had not been there in the first place. The principal charge against MacSwiney was based on one of the latter documents.[185] He was court marshalled and sentenced to two years' imprisonment in Brixton Prison, in England.

In protest against his imprisonment, MacSwiney immediately began a hunger strike. The deputy Lord Mayor of Cork, Councillor Donal O'Callaghan, asked for and received permission for Fr Dominic to accompany the Lady Mayoress to England on 20 August 1920. When they arrived at Brixton Prison, Fr Dominic said that they found him to be 'wan, wasted and haggard looking, but clear in mind and fully determined to force open the gates of his prison, even though he should die in the attempt'.[186] Coincidently, MacSwiney was in the same prison ward where another Irish nationalist, Sir Roger Casement (1864-1916), had been imprisoned while on remand in Brixton Prison.

Statements in the British press alleged that the Lord Mayor was taking food and was able to be up and about. Fr Dominic said that these rumours were all absolutely false. He attested that the Lord Mayor never had any food from the evening of his illegal arrest until he became unconscious. Up to then he 'had a desire for food and said that he would give £1,000 for a cup of tea'.[187] He also added that 'he never complained, never flickered and knew that he was risking a slow, lingering death and was ready for it'.

Fr Dominic recorded that MacSwiney often spoke of how helpful his religion had been to him and spoke 'in loving admiration of Tomás MacCurtain and Eoghan Ruadh O'Neill (1590-1649) and of the magnificent combination in them of the qualities of a soldier and a Catholic'. He asked to be buried in the rough brown habit of the Third Order[188] so that he might form a fourth with MacCurtain, O'Neill and Joan of Arc, who were also members of the Third Order. Joan of Arc, a French Catholic folk heroine, was known as the Maid of Orleans. MacSwiney said, 'our fight is her fight all over again'.[189] Eoghan Ruadh O'Neill, a nephew of Hugh O'Neill, was a distinguished soldier in the Spanish Army.

Fig. 60. 'Le Martyr Irlandais', Terence MacSwiney on his death bed, ministered to by Fr Dominic O'Connor OFM Cap., *Le Petit Journal*, 19 September 1920. (Irish Capuchin Provincial Archives, Dublin)

He returned to Ireland in 1642, to aid the leaders who had formed the Catholic Confederation.

MacSwiney's hunger strike attracted worldwide press attention. This resulted in workers downing tools in New York, riots in the streets of Barcelona, mass demonstrations from Boston to Buenos Aires and a threat by the United States of America of a boycott of English goods. As a consequence, Ireland's War of Independence also became international news. Fr Dominic ministered to MacSwiney throughout his seventy-four days of hunger strike and was present at his death in Brixton Prison. On 19 September 1920, a drawing on the front page of the French magazine *Le Petit Journal* depicted Fr Dominic praying at the death bed of '*le martyr Irlandais*', Terence MacSwiney (Fig. 60). Fr Dominic gave an account of the last days of MacSwiney and recorded that:

> His suffering no pen could write. Try and conceive the pain you suffer in your shoulders and in your back and in your knees, the stiff, numbing, pain in the calves of your legs, the agony in your heels, instep and ankles, even if you remain for six hours outstretched on your back. What a relief to bend your knees and draw them up toward your body. But even that little relief our heroic sufferer could not have, for the flesh had wasted from his knee.[190]

Before his body was returned to Cork, a requiem Mass was held for McSwiney in Southwark Cathedral in London, offici- ated by Archbishop Daniel Mannix (1864-1963). This Mass has been immortalised in a painting by Sir John Lavery (1856-1941), entitled 'Funeral of Terence MacSwiney', 1920 (Fig.61). Lavery also painted a portrait of the 'Lady Mayoress, Mrs. Terence MacSwiney' 1920, and both paintings are in the Crawford Gallery in Cork.

Fig. 61. 'The Funeral of Terence MacSwiney', 1920 by Sir John Lavery (1856-1941).
(Crawford Art Gallery, Cork)

Fr Dominic was arrested in 1920, on his return from England, and taken to Dublin Castle where he was court-marshalled and sentenced to five years' imprisonment. During his time in Pankhurst Prison in England, he became acquainted with two notable republican detainees, Ernie O'Malley (1897-1957) and Pádraig Ó Caoimh. O'Malley was commander of the anti-Treaty IRA in the Four Courts, Dublin, during the Civil War. O'Caoimh was an officer with the Cork Brigade of the IRA and was later Secretary General of the GAA (1929-64). Following the signing of the Treaty in 1921, Fr Dominic was released on a general amnesty, in January 1922.

On 25 February 1922, Fr Dominic was granted the freedom of Cork. His citation read:

As a mark of respect for his valuable services rendered as chaplain to the first two republican Lord Mayors of Cork and especially for his steadfast dedication to Toirdhealbach MacSuibhne T.D. while suffering and dying for his country in Brixton Prison and as a mark of appreciation of his own suffering in Ireland's cause.

In spite of outside protests and internal misgivings, about the activities of some of their members, the Capuchin Order reconciled its differences with Fr Dominic. There is a plaque, on the interior south wall of Holy Trinity church, which commemorates Fr Dominic O'Connor OFM Cap., Brigade Chaplain IRA, 1916-21.

However, not everyone in the Order was happy with the involvement of its members in the nationalist movement. In an address to his community, in February 1917, Fr Thomas Dowling said:

> Loyalty to the Order and the Community, to which we are assigned by obedience, has always been a salient feature of Capuchin life … The standard of our conduct is clearly set out for us in the Pastoral Letter of our Father General 'the friars shall keep themselves aloof from political factions but should be gentle and peaceful with all in accordance with the mind of our Seraphic Father, St. Francis'. When members have strong views on certain questions it is difficult to conceal them but we are untrue to the first principle of religious life if we barter this loyalty to our Order and Community for the sake of idealistic individuals. I would not be true to my position if I did not point out that this Community has earned the unenviable reputation of not being all it should be in this respect … During the long history of our Province as a separate entity, no more painful incident has occurred than that interference of our internal

governance that occurred recently, when our Superior
General reproved us for implicating ourselves in Politics …
If we are to avoid ruin, we must eschew Politics altogether
from our public attitudes.[191]

In spite of admonishments, some Capuchins continued to provide support to the nationalist movement at the onset of the
Civil War. In June 1922, the Four Courts, located close to the
Capuchin Friary in Church Street, Dublin, came under siege
from Free-State forces. Fr Dominic O'Connor, assisted by
Fr Albert Bibby, was in the Four Courts ministering to the IRA
garrison, commanded by Ernie O'Malley, as it was shelled by
Free-State artillery. They provided spiritual comfort and assisted
in the evacuation of the wounded from there and subsequently
facilitated the surrender of the defeated garrison.[192] Fr Dominic

Fig. 62
Fr Dominic O'Connor
OFM Cap. at the Four
Courts, Dublin. *Illustrated
London News*, 8 July 1922.

WEARING THE RED CROSS : FATHER DOMINIC, WHO
WAS REPORTED TO HAVE BEEN WITH THE REBELS
IN THE FOUR COURTS.

was escorted away from the Four Courts by Free-State troops after its capture in 1922 (Fig. 62).

Subsequently, both Fr Dominic and Fr Albert were sent to the Capuchin Mission in the United States of America. Fr Dominic was sent to Bend in Oregon, where he died on 17 October 1933. Oregon was also the place where his uncle, Fr Luke Sheehan OSFC, had been a pioneer of the Capuchin Mission several years beforehand. Fr Albert was sent to Santa Inez in California, where he died on 14 February 1925. On 12 August 1922, Fr Albert wrote to Fr Juan Antonio de San Juan en Persiceto, Minister General of the Capuchin Order, claiming that 'this decision would seem to be part of the penalisation which has been meted out to me, probably because of my activity during the period of hostility in Dublin last summer'. He went on to declare his 'absolute impartiality' during the War of Independence and later at the outbreak of Civil War hostilities in Dublin in 1922.[193] Fr Dominic seems to have maintained his sense of humour as he showed in a letter to Fr Edwin Fitzgibbon. On 8 December 1927, Fr Dominic detailed the progress of building works in his ministry in Oregon and wrote:

> As soon as the weather moderates, I will begin the building of the church at Pilot Rock. I intended to call it Santa Clara but I will get a donation of $1,000 if I call it St. Agnes. What's in a name? I've been called many names myself, few of them as complimentary in the change as this one.[194]

On 14 June 1958, the remains of Fr Dominic and Fr Albert were repatriated to Ireland. This was achieved through the efforts of the Remains Repatriation Committee of the Cork No. 1 Brigade, Old IRA. Florence O'Donoghue (1895-1967), Head of Intelligence for the Cork Brigade during the War of Independence, was appointed Honorary Secretary of the committee and Cornelius Neenan was appointed the committee's representative in the United States of America. The repatriation was a torturous affair, which was stalled by the outbreak of the Second World War. Aside from the financial difficulties, the committee also had to contend with a certain reluctance on the part of Church authorities. Ultimately, a State funeral was held for the two priests at which President Sean T. O'Kelly (1882-1966), Taoiseach Eamon de Valera and other members of the government attended. O'Kelly was a member of the Gaelic League and had been imprisoned for his part in the Easter Rising of 1916. He was one of the first to join Fianna Fail and served two terms as President of Ireland (1948-59). Fr Hilary McDonagh OFM Cap., Vicar Provincial of the Irish Capuchins, was the principal celebrant and Dr Cornelius Lucey (1902-82), Bishop of Cork, also officiated at the Mass. The funeral procession for the two priests was a very public affair, as can be seen from a photograph in June 1958 from the *Cork Examiner* (Fig. 63). This shows the funeral cortege as it passed over the bridge, into Anglesea Street in Cork, on its way to the cemetery at Rochestown, outside the city.

The two priests were buried with full military honours, as Irish patriots. Both are now interred at the Capuchin Friary, Rochestown, just outside Cork City. This is attached to Rochestown College (Fig. 64), which was founded in 1884 by the Capuchin Order. Based on a model at Ponte a Poppi in Tuscany, Italy, it was set up as a centre of training and a novitiate for young Capuchins. It is interesting to note, it is alleged that Captain Robert Monteith (1880-1956), Officer in charge of the Irish Brigade who accompanied Roger Casement in bringing German weapons to Ireland via Banna Strand, County Kerry in 1916, and later Liam Mellows (1895-1920), the Irish republican and Sinn Féin politician, both found shelter in the Rochestown Friary when they were 'on the run'. Since the introduction of free education in Ireland, in the early 1970s, it has become a secondary school called after St Francis.

In 1959, the veterans of Na Fianna Eireann unveiled a memorial to the two patriot priests, Fr Dominic and Fr Albert, in the grounds of the Capuchin Hostel in Raheny, Dublin. Na Fianna Eireann was founded by Bulmer Hobson (1883-1969) in the early 1900s as an Irish national boy scouts movement. Hobson was also a leading member of the Irish Volunteers and the Irish Republican Brotherhood before the Easter Rising 1916, which he opposed. This monument is a life-sized Calvary, in re-constituted stone, modelled by the Neff Brothers of Cork. It was donated by Eamonn Martin (1892-1971), former Chief of Staff of Na Fianna Éireann. This was an organisation in which the two priests were keenly interested.[195]

It should be noted as well that many members of the Capuchin Order also served with the British Army during the First World War. For example, Fr Ignatius Collins OFM Cap. (1885-1961). He was the son of Captain Jeremiah Collins, of the Cork Harbour Board, and was born in Cotter Street in Cork. He was educated at the Seraphic College in Rochestow, County Cork, where, by all accounts, he was an outstanding scholar. He entered the Capuchin Order and was ordained a priest in 1910. He took his BA

Fig. 63. Cortege for the repatriation of the remains of Fr Dominic O'Connor OFM Cap. and Fr Albert Bibby OFM Cap. crossing into Anglesea Street, Cork, 1958. (Cork Examiner)

Fig. 64. The Capuchin college, friary and church, Rochestown, County Cork.
(Irish Capuchin Provincial Archives, Dublin)

in Philosophy at the Royal University and was awarded a Doctorate in Theology and Philosophy from the Gregorian University in Rome. Fr Ignatius responded to the call of Cardinal Francis Bourne, Archbishop of Westminster, seeking Catholic priests to act as chaplains in the British forces. He was sent to France in 1915 and acted as chaplain with the 69th Field Ambulance Corps. During the First World War, his Division served on the Western Front and participated in many major offences, including the Battles of the Somme and Messines. In October 1917, the Division was transferred to the Italian Front. In January 1918, Fr Collins was awarded the Military Cross and was promoted to the rank of major. His awards also include the Italian War Cross of Merit (Fig. 65). After the war, he initially returned to the Rochestown Friary in County Cork. In 1922, he was elected Guardian of the Capuchin Friary in Kilkenny. In 1943, he was transferred to Dublin where he died on 21 October 1961.

There is no specific reason why so many members of the Capuchin Order became involved with Irish nationalism. They did this at a time when many other priests were unwilling to get involved or even to minister to those associated with the 1916 Rising and subsequent Civil War. They also did this in spite of admonishments from inside and outside the Capuchin Order.

One can speculate that members of the Capuchin Order became involved in the nationalist movement as they were driven by a desire to minister to people who were deeply religious and to whom a Catholic presence, particularly at the time of death, was paramount. As Fr Dominic said, 'to help the souls of the soldiers'. It could also be speculated that their involvement was due to the influence of the Gaelic League and its aspiration for an Irish Ireland. At the time, many members of the Capuchin Order were attracted to this ideal and an independent Ireland would have been, for many of them, a logical next step.

Fig. 65. Fr Ignatius Collins OFM Cap. and the medals awarded to him during the First World War. (Irish Capuchin Provincial Archives, Dublin)

Conclusion

The building of Holy Trinity church evolved over many years due to a number of factors in its chequered history. The story is steeped in the history of Cork and the Capuchin Order in Ireland. It stands today as a result of the vision of its patron, Fr Theobald Mathew, and the efforts of his many successors. It was built at a time of a renaissance in ecclesiastical architecture in post-Emancipation Ireland, which embraced both Gothic Revival and Neo-Classical styles.

The original Gothic Revival design for the church was by George R. Pain, a noted English architect in the 1800s. His design has been somewhat modified by the truncation of the spire, in its final manifestation. Nevertheless, it still remains true to his original intentions. It could be argued that his original design, with its soaring spire, would have added more impact to the building and the Cork City skyline. Notwithstanding this, the distinctive Gothic Revival portico and steeple are iconic landmarks in Cork.

The main reasons for the delay in finishing Holy Trinity church were problems with its foundations, a court case with the architect, raising sufficient money for the project, the beginning of the temperance crusade and the Great Famine. The prolonged nature of its completion was not unusual, given the turbulent history of Ireland over the period. For example, and probably for similar reasons, St Mary's (Dominican) church in Cork took twenty-nine years to complete and the St Augustine and John's church in Dublin took thirty-seven years, to be completed. The original design for Holy Trinity church was not fully executed, which again was not unusual for the time. For example, St Mary's (Dominican) church in Cork was to have had two western towers, one on either side of the front of the church, which were never built,[196] presumably due to cost factors.

The early use of cast-iron in building Holy Trinity church is probably attributable to the problems encountered with its foundations. Clearly, cast-iron columns were a considerable improvement on stone columns when it came to load bearing on marshy foundations.

The interior of the church has been completely altered and is now unrecognisable from its original design by William Atkins. It does, however, have some magnificent stained-glass windows. Two of these were made by the Harry Clarke Studio and the third, to Harry Clarke's design and under his close supervision, by J. Clarke & Sons Studio. These windows are not currently in the *Gazetteer of Irish Stained Glass* and should be recognised in the official canon of Harry Clarke's work. The renowned expert on Harry Clarke, Dr Nicola Gordon Bowe, has agreed that a compelling case has been made for this oversight. On 3 May 1929, Harry Clarke wrote in a letter to Monseigneur Walsh 'my work is not always popular but people do look at it, even if they dislike it they are interested – most glass is mentally digested in a minute'.[197] Whatever Harry's feelings were about his work, his stained-glass windows in Holy Trinity church are clearly an ornament to the city.

The contribution of the Capuchin Order to both Cork City and Ireland has been immeasurable. This is manifested through charitable and social work as well as cultural and civil activities. The involvement of members of the Capuchin Order, during the turbulent times of Irish nationalism, was outstanding as they ministered to those involved when many churchmen were not willing to do so. This contribution has been somewhat neglected over the years and will undoubtedly be recognised during the forthcoming centenary commemoration of the 1916 Rising and the subsequent granting of Irish independence.

The charismatic leadership of Fr Mathew was the main driving force in commissioning Holy Trinity church. He also started a social revolution that resulted in the establishment of temperance societies in every parish in the country. It could be argued that the latter changed the way Irish people came to see themselves, rather than simply as victims of poverty, degradation and foreign domination. There is no doubt that it also helped to change the stereotype of the 'drunken Irish Paddy'. Fr Mathew's upbringing was different from Irish Catholics and his seminary training was also different from that of secular priests. This probably accounts for his good and bad points, in the eyes of his followers and detractors, as well as the respect in which he was held by many. He was a man before his time as well as a courageous, charitable, innovative and stubborn one. Eventually, through the work of his many successors, the church has become a permanent monument to his memory and to all the subsequent members of the Capuchin Order who followed in his footsteps.

While little has been written about Holy Trinity church, it is an iconic building in Cork City due to its landmark location, its charismatic patron and its social and historic connections. On 8 June 1982, the *Cork Examiner* described it as 'the most artistically designed and functionally suitable church in Cork and perhaps in the country'. This is undoubtedly an exaggeration, but nevertheless, Holy Trinity is a much-loved church that holds a special affection in the hearts of Cork people.

Notes

1   Revd Fr Augustine, OFM Cap., *Footprints of Fr Mathew OFM Cap* (M.H. Gill & Son; Dublin, 1947), p. 20
2   Cork City Library
3   T.F. McNamara, *Portrait of Cork* (Watermans; Cork, 1981), p. 15
4   Ibid., p. 15
5   McNamara, *Portrait of Cork*, p. 61
6   Kieran McCarthy, 'Cork Heritage', http://corkheritage.ie/?page.id=980 27/02/2013
7   Henry Allen Jefferies, *Cork – Historical Perspectives* (Four Courts Press; Dublin, 2004), p. 168
8   McCarthy, 'Cork Heritage'
9   Allen Jefferies, *Cork – Historical Perspectives*, p. 191
10 Fr Thomas Larkin OFM Cap., 'The Capuchins in Cork', *The Capuchin Annual* (1976), p. 174
11 John Windele & James Coleman, *Historical & Descriptive Nature of the City of Cork From its Foundation to the Middle of the 19th Century* (Written 1837 and revised, abridged and annotated by James Coleman 1930, Hon. Sec. Cork Historical & Archaeological Society) (Guy & Co. Ltd; Cork, 1930), p. 46
12 Fr F.X. Martin OSA, *Friar Nugent – A Study of Francis Lavalin Nugent, Agent of the Counter-Reformation* (Capuchin Historical Institute; Rome and Methuen & Co. Ltd; London, 1966)
13 Ibid.
14 'A Brief History of the Irish Capuchins', Irish Capuchin Provincial Archives, Dublin.
15 Analectat Vol. XLVII 1898, p. 221, Irish Capuchin Provincial Archives, Dublin.
16 Fr Senan OFM Cap. (ed.), *Capuchin Annual* (Dublin, 1932), p. 158
17 Revd T.J. Walsh OFM Cap., 'The Capuchins in Cork', *Capuchin Annual* (1952)

18 Senan, *Capuchin Annual,* p. 159

19 Larkin, 'The Capuchins in Cork', p. 175

20 Senan, *Capuchin Annual,* p. 159

21 John F. Quinn, *Fr Mathew's Crusade – Temperance in 19th Century Ireland and Irish America* (University of Mass. Press, Amhurst & Boston, 2002), p. 39

22 Ibid., p. 39

23 Revd Patrick Rogers, *Fr Theobald Mathew – Apostle of Temperance* (Browne & Nolan Ltd; Dublin, 1943), pp. 1-5

24 John Francis Maguire MP, *Fr Mathew – A Biography* (Eason & Son; Dublin). Edited and abridged by Rosa Mulholland; *Centenary Year of the Temperance Movement,* p. 1

25 Quinn, *Fr Mathew's Crusade,* p. 39

26 Revd Patrick Rogan, *Fr Theobald Mathew – Apostle of Temperance* (The Catholic Book Club; London, 1945), p. 10

27 Rogers, *Fr Theobald Mathew,* p. 5

28 Rogan, *Fr Theobald Mathew,* p. 17

29 Rogers, *Fr Theobald Mathew,* p. 19

30 Augustine, OFM Cap., *Footprints of Fr Mathew OFM Cap,* p. 83-4

31 Rogan, *Fr Theobald Mathew,* p. 31

32 F.S., 'Fr Mathew & Temperance', *Capuchin Annual* (1930)

33 Rogan, *Fr Theobald Mathew,* p. 31

34 F.S., 'Fr Mathew & Temperance', *Capuchin Annual* (1930)

35 Irish Capuchin Provincial Archives – Note in Fr Thomas Dowling papers in connection with the Fr Mathew Pavilion at the Cork Exhibition 1902/3

36 Colm Kerrigan, *Fr Mathew & the Irish Temperance Movement, 1838-49* (Cork University Press; Cork, 1992), p. 6

37 www.libraryireland.com/biography/TheobaldMathew/php 14/02/2014

38 The Book of the Community 1893, Ref. No. 207/190, Irish Capuchin Provincial Archives, Church Street, Dublin

39 Rogers, *Fr Theobald Mathew,* pp. 1-5

40 Augustine, OFM Cap., *Footprints of Fr Mathew OFM Cap,* p. 145

41 Ibid., p. 555-6

42 *London Illustrated News,* Vol. 111, 30 October 1843, p. 321

43 Maguire was M.P. for Dungarvan and then Cork City and several times Lord Mayor of Cork City. He founded the Cork Gas Co. and subsequently, in 1841, the *Cork Examiner*

44 Irish Capuchin Provincial Archives, Dublin Ref. Ul/40/2/049

45 National Gallery of Ireland, Dublin Ref. 4035 – purchased 1971

46 David Lee, *James Pain – Architect* (Limerick civic Trust; Limerick, 2005), p. 133-4

47 Rogers, *Fr Theobald Mathew,* p. 27

48 Revd James Coombes, 'Catholic Churches in the 19th Century; Some Newspaper Sources', *Journal of the Cork Historical and Archaeological Society,*

Part 1, Vol. LXXXl, No. 231 (Cork, January – June 1975)

49   Frederick O'Dwyer, *The Architecture of Deane & Woodward* (Cork University Press; Cork, 1997), p. 130

50   Brendan Grimes, 'The Architecture of Dublin's Neo-Classical Roman Catholic Temples 1803-62' PhD Thesis (Faculty of History of Art & Design & Complimentary Studies, NCAD; Dublin, 2005), p. 24

51   Mark Bence-Jones, 'Two Pairs of Architectural Brothers, Cork 11', *Country Life* (August, 1967)

52   Ibid.

53   O'Dwyer, *The Architecture of Deane & Woodward*, p. 12

54   Senan, *Capuchin Annual*, p. 158

55   Augustine, OFM Cap., *Footprints of Fr Mathew OFM Cap*, p. 81-2

56   Fr Stanislaus OSFC, Historical Jottings Re the Church of the Most Holy Trinity (Fr Mathew's Chapel), Irish Capuchin Provincial Archives, Dublin

57   Augustine, OFM Cap., *Footprints of Fr Mathew OFM Cap*, p. 80

58   Edward McParland, 'Church or Chapel? The Case of St. Mary's Church, Pope's Quay Cork' in Raymond Gillespie & R.F. Foster (eds), *Irish Provincial Cultures in the Long 18th Century – Making the Middle Sort, Essays for Toby Bernard* (Four Courts Press; Dublin, 2012), p. 234

59   IAA Accession No. 0086/073 Model, 1825, 780 c 240 x 145

60   Senan, *Capuchin Annual*, p. 158

61   Stanislaus OSFC, Historical Jottings

62   Augustine, OFM Cap., *Footprints of Fr Mathew OFM Cap*, pp. 81-2

63   Stanislaus OSFC, Historical Jottings

64   Augustine, OFM Cap., *Footprints of Fr Mathew OFM Cap*, p. 80

65   www.historyplace.org/worldhistory/famine/hunger.htm 19/01/2013

66   The Oratory Leaflet, 8/12/2006 – Irish Capuchin Provincial Archives, Dublin

67   Ibid.

68   Augustine, OFM Cap., *Footprints of Fr Mathew OFM Cap*, p. 82

69   The only reference found on his interior says that 'the high wooden ceiling was make of pine, coloured red to imitate oak' spacing http://www.iaa.ie/view/282/building/CO+CORK%2C+FATHER 25/10/2012

70   Anon., News Gleanings 1890, notebook, Irish Capuchin Provincial Archives, Dublin.

71   National Gallery of Ireland, Dublin

72   Grimes, 'The Architecture of Dublin's Neo-Classical Roman Catholic Temples 1803-62', p. 31

73   Anon., Cork Friary, notebook, Irish Capuchin Provincial Archives, Dublin Ref. 223-5

74   News Gleanings 1890, Irish Capuchin Provincial Archives, Dublin

75   Revd Paul Neary OFM Cap., Analystic Biographical History of Irish Province c1919 Ref. 194/195, Irish Capuchin Provincial Archives, Church Street, Dublin

76   Ibid., Ref. 198/9

77   *Irish Builder*, No. 32 (1890), p. 155

78   Jeremy Williams, *A Companion Guide to Architecture in Ireland 1837-1921* (Irish Academic Press; Dublin, 1999), pp. 59-60

79   Neary OFM Cap., Analystic Biographical History of Irish Province c1919

80   Ibid., Ref. 203

81   Ibid., Ref. 203

82   Stanislaus OSFC, Historical Jottings

83   News Gleanings 1890, Irish Capuchin Provincial Archives, Dublin.

84   Neary OFM Cap., Analystic Biographical History of Irish Province c1919.

85   Matthew J. McDermott, *Ireland's Architectural Heritage – An Outline History of Irish Architecture* (Folens & Co. Ltd; Dublin, 1975), p. 101

86   Michael J. Lewis, *The Gothic Revival* (Thames & Hudson; London, 2002), pp. 80-9

87   Megan Adrich, *Gothic Revival* (Phaidon Press; London, 1997), p. 69

88   Brian de Breffni & George Mott, *The Churches & Abbeys of Ireland* (Hudson Ltd; London, 1976), p. 153

89   Christine Casey, *The Buildings of Ireland – Dublin* (Yale University Press; New Haven & New York, 2005), pp. 627-8

90   Ibid., p. 154

91   David Lee, *Georgian Limerick 1714-1845*, *Vol. 1*, David Lee & Christine Gonzales (eds) (Limerick Civic Trust & FAS; Limerick, 2000), p. 249

92   McDonald, *Ireland's Architectural Heritage*, p. 127

93   Edward Diestalkamp, 'Building Techniques & Architecture' Paper given at the Georgian Group symposium, published as *Late Georgian Classicism* (1987), p. 74

94   Ibid., p. 74

95   McDonald, *Ireland's Architectural Heritage – An Outline History of Irish Architecture*, p. 135

96   Ibid., p. 138

97   Stephen Parissien, 'A Brief Guide to Georgian Iron-work', *The Georgian Group Guide No. 8* (Dent; England, n.d.), p. 4

98   Michael McCarthy, *Studies in the History of Art* (Four Courts Press; Dublin, 2005), p. 19

99   Williams, *A Companion Guide to Architecture in Ireland 1837-1921*, p. 60

100   OS Survey of Ireland, Map of Cork City 1841, OSI40/41 sheet 23, scale 1:1056, National Archives of Ireland, Dublin

101   News Gleanings 1890, Irish Capuchin Provincial Archives, Dublin, pp. 59-60

102   Senan, *Capuchin Annual*, p. 158

103   There is some dispute about the date this company was founded, which has not been resolved, with dates given as diverse as 1813 and 1837

104   Martin Harrison, *Victorian Stained Glass* (Barne & Jenkins; London, 1980), pp. 77-78. Charles Alexander (C.A.) Gibbs (1825-77), Alexander Gibbs (1832-86) and Isaac Alexander Gibbs Jnr. (1849-99). The latter established his own company, E.A. Gibbs & Howard, in the late 1870s. His partner was William Morris Howard (b. 1856). The firm continued after the death of Gibbs, under Howard, until 1918

105 J.J. Walsh, 'The Capuchins in Ireland', *Capuchin Annual* (1952)

106 Br Benvenutus, 'Valuable Paper Cuttings – Referring chiefly to Cork Friary & Church in the Early 80s of the 19th Century' (collected when he was a student), Irish Capuchin Provincial Archives, Dublin

107 Stanislaus OSFC, Historical Jottings

108 This is based on a general perception that the windows came from Glasgow as well as a comment in Jeremy Williams *A Companion Guide to Architecture in Ireland 1827-1921* (Irish Academic Press; Dublin, 1994), p. 60, which has a mis-attribution to the O'Connell Memorial window to Hemmings of Newcastle. Therefore it was logical to check if this might have been the artist for these two stained-glass windows instead

109 Joyce Little, *Stained Glass, Marks & Monograms* (National Association of Decorative & Fine Art Society; London, 2002)

110 Theo Snoddy, *Dictionary of Irish Artists – 20th Century* (Merlin Publishing, 2006)

111 Ibid.

112 http://dib.cambridge.org//viewFullScreen.do?filename=/app/dib/production/content/html/9 17/10/2012

113 Fr Nessan Shaw OFM Cap., *The Irish Capuchins – Record of a Century 1885-1989* (Capuchin Publications; Dublin, 1985), p. 73

114 Sara Purser (1848-1943) and other *An Tur Gloine* artists also have stained-glass windows in this church. They were commissioned by Sir John O'Connell who was anxious to promote the work of Irish stained-glass artists, as most of such work was imported from abroad at the time

115 TCD Ms. Library Ref. 5981 284

116 TCD Ms. Library Ref. 5981 352

117 TCD Ms. Library Ref. 5981 489

118 Nicola Gordon Bowe, *The Life & Work of Harry Clarke* (Irish Academic Press; Dublin, 1989), p. 143

119 Ibid., p. 260

120 TCD Ms. Library Ref. 5981 617

121 TCD Ms. Library Ref. 5981 637

122 TCD Ms. Library Ref. 5981 823

123 TCD Ms. Library Ref. 5981 342

124 TCD Ms. Library Ref. 5981 860

125 TCD Ms. Library Ref. Order Book 1, p. 143, 28 June 1916 – in the middle of 1918 orders

126 TCD Ms. Library Ref. 5981 868

127 TCD Ms. Library Ref. 5981 943

128 TCD Manuscript (Ms.) Library Ref. 5981 942

129 TCD Ms. Library Ref. 5981 966

130 Gordon Bowe, *The Life & Work of Harry Clarke*, p. 312. Gordon Bowe outlines that 'where (A) follows the title of the window, this means that Clarke was actively involved in part of the window's execution, the rest being executed under his supervision in the Clarke Studio. Where (B) follows the title, this

means that it was initially conceived and designed by him but executed by the Clarke Studio under his close supervision.' A similar categorisation is also used by Lucy Costigan & Michael Cullen, who updated the Gazeteer of Irish Stained Glass in *Strangest Genius: The Stained Glass of Harry Clarke* (The History Press of Ireland; Dublin, 2010)

131 Gordon Bowe, *The Life & Work of Harry Clarke*, p. 144

132 In 1945, a split occurred in the Irish trade union movement when a number of Irish-based unions disaffiliated from the Irish Congress of Trade Unions and formed a new congress called Congress of Irish Unions. This was mirrored in Cork when some members disaffiliated from the Cork Workers Council and formed the Cork Council of Trade Unions. In 1960, the two Cork bodies agreed to form the present-day Cork Council of Trade Unions

133 Their address was Highcliffe, Connaoght Avenue, Cork and Mrs O'Donovan died on 12 August 1932

134 Gordon Bowe, *The Life & Work of Harry Clarke*, also mentions these windows: 'the Franciscans in Cork ordered two further windows, a Sacred Heart with attendant saints and an Immaculate Conception, both two lights', p. 272; TCD Ms. Library Ref. 5981 352

135 Note in Holy Trinity church, Cork by Fr Martin OFM Cap. Dated 12 January 1933

136 TCD Ms. Library Ref. 5998 633

137 TCD Ms. Library Ref. 5998 654

138 TCD Ms. Library Ref. 5998 692

139 TCD Ms. Library Ref. 5998 738

140 TCD Ms. Library Ref. 5998 775

141 TCD Ms. Library Ref. 5998 941

142 TCD Ms. Library Ref. 6000

143 TCD Ms. Library Ref. 5999 797

144 TCD Ms. Library Ref. 5999 873

145 TCD Ms. Library Ref. 5999 896

146 TCD Ms. Library Ref. 5999 953

147 TCD Ms. Library Order Book 2, p. 12, dated 12 January 1927, Order No. 151

148 TCD Ms. Library Order Book 2, p. 13, dated 26 January 1927, Order No. 1518

149 TCD Ms Library Ref. 11182/495

150 TCD Ms. Library Ref. 11182/680

151 He worked in the studios during Harry Clarke's lifetime and sadly ended up in Grange Gorman in 1929, due to manic depression. The attribution is written in pencil, with a question mark, at the base of each drawing

152 TCD Ms. Library Ref. 11182/681

153 TCD Ms. Library Ref. 5998/692. Gordon Bowe also mentions these two windows and outlines that 'these had been carried out, as had the earlier window, Harry's design', Nicola Gordon Bowe 'The Life & Work of Harry Clarke (1889-1931) Vol. 1-3', Thesis (TCD, 1981), p. 764

154 James White & Michael Wynne, *Irish Stained Glass – A Catalogue of Irish Stained Glass Windows by Irish Artists in the 20th Century* (Gill & MacMillan in association with The Furrow; Dublin, 1963)

155 Gordon Bowe, *The Life & Work of Harry Clarke*, p. 68

156 Nicola Gordon Bowe, 'Symbolism in Turn of the Century Irish Art', *Irish Arts Review* (Dublin, 1989/90), pp. 133-4

157 Our Lady's Chapel, Terenure church, Dublin by Harry Clarke in 1924

158 Chapel of the Oblate Fathers, Belcamp Hall, Raheny, County Dublin by Harry Clarke in 1925

159 St Barrahane's church, Castletownsend, County Cork by Harry Clarke in 1920

160 From his book *Nos Eglisesi*

161 Coincidently, they were the same architects for the St Augustin & John's church in Dublin whose design was also influenced by Peterborough Cathedral

162 This involved the celebrant of the Mass facing the congregation rather than conducting the service with his back to the congregation as was the custom heretofore

163 Minutes of church records

164 Ibid.

165 Booklet on the re-opening and blessing of Holy Trinity church 1982, Irish Capuchin Provincial Archives, Dublin

166 Neary OFM Cap., Analystic Biographical History of Irish Province c1919, Ref. 230/214

167 It is interesting to note that there is a similar wooden reredos altar, carved by the same company, in the chapel of St Kieran's College, Kilkenny

168 www.jesuit.ie/2012-06-08-16-42-53/history-of-the-irish-province?thewall=18: 4/11/2013

169 Fr Pascal Larkin, OFM Cap., 'The Capuchins in Cork', *Capuchin Annual* (1976), p. 176

170 Susan Schreibman, 'Introduction to the Capuchin Annual', The Thomas MacGreevy Archive, 1999 http://www.macgreevy.org/styles=text&source=com. cpa.xml&action=show 10/11/2012

171 www.dublincitypubliclibrary.ie/story/capuchin-annual-dublin 30/3/2014

172 Daniel Breen & Dan Spalding, *The Cork International Exhibition 1902 and 1903 A Snapshot of Edwardian Cork* (Irish Academic Press; Sallins, Co. Kildare, 2014), p. 180

173 Ibid., p. 187. This was named after Sir Edward Fitzgerald (1846-1927), Lord Mayor of Cork, who instigated and promoted the Cork International Exhibition 1902 and 1903

174 Irish Capuchin Provincial Archives, Dublin

175 *Capuchin Annual* (1942), p. 320

176 Irish Capuchin Provincial Archives, Dublin

177 Senan, *Capuchin Annual*, p. 211

178 Fr Henry OFM Cap. (ed.), *Capuchin Annual* (1966), p. 273

179 A Passionist Order Church in Dublin

180 Irish Capuchin Provincial Archives, Dublin – CA/IR/1/1/2/2/4

181 Irish Capuchin Provincial Archives, Dublin – CA/IR/1/5/13

182 Irish Capuchin Provincial Archives, Dublin – CA/IR/1/5/4/3

183 Fr Henry OFM Cap. (ed.), *Capuchin Annual* (1966), p. 170

184 Irish Capuchin Provincial Archives, Dublin – CA/IR/1/5/2/1

185 Fr Senan OFM Cap. (ed.), *Capuchin Annual* (1942), p. 337

186 Ibid., p. 320

187 Ibid., p. 340

188 The Third Order of St Francis is a lay confraternity of Catholic men and women, both married and single, who live their lives following a Rule of Life like that of St Francis

189 Senan, *Capuchin Annual* (1942), p. 340

190 Irish Capuchin Provincial Archives, Dublin – CA/IR/1/5/2/14 also *Capuchin Annual* (1942) pp. 337-42

191 Irish Capuchin Provincial Archives, Dublin – copy in Fr Thomas Dowling papers

192 www.iar.ie/4degi/f?Capuchin.Revolution

193 Irish Capuchin Provincial Archives, Dublin – CA/IR/1/1/2/4/6

194 Irish Capuchin Provincial Archives, Dublin – CA/IR/1/5/4/6

195 Irish Capuchin Provincial Archives, Dublin – CA/IR/1/9/3

196 McParland, 'Church or Chapel?', p. 231. The foundation stone for this neo-Classical church building was laid in 1832, it opened for services in 1839 but the portico was not added until 1861

197 TCD Ms. Library Ref. 5998

Bibliography

Aldrich, Megan, *Gothic Revival* (Phaidon Press; London, 1997)

Augustine OFM Cap., Revd Fr, *Footprints of Fr Matthew OFM Cap.* (M.H. Gill & Son; Dublin, 1947)

Br Benvenutus, *Valuable Paper Cuttings Referring Chiefly to Cork Friary & Church in Early 80s of Nineteenth Century*, collected by Br Benvenutus when a student (Irish Capuchin Provincial Archives, Dublin)

Bence-Jones, Mark, 'Two Pairs of Architectural Brothers, Cork II', *Country Life*, August 1967

Bergdall, Barry, *European Architecture 1750-1890* (Oxford Press, Oxford, 2000)

Breen, Daniel & Spalding, Tom, *The Cork International Exhibition 1902/1903 – A Snapshot of Edwardian Cork*, (Irish Academic Press; Sallins, County Kildare, 2014)

Brownlee, David B., *The Law Courts – The Architecture of George Edmund Street* (The Architectural Historical Foundation & MIT; Boston, 1984)

British Society of Master Glass Producers http://flickr.com/photos/davewebster14/sets/72157619489136162/with/3536192314/ 18/03/13

Casey, Christine, *The Buildings of Ireland – Dublin* (Yale University Press; New Haven & London, 2005)

Clarke, Maureen, 'St. Francis Xavier Church, Gardiner St., Dublin', *Irish Arts Review*, Vol. 1, 1998

Coombes, Revd James, 'Catholic Churches in the 19th Century – Some Newspaper Sources', *Cork Historical & Architectural Society*, Vol. LXXl, No. 231, January-June 1975

Corish, Patrick J. Ed., *The History of Irish Catholicism – The Church Since Emancipation* – Vol. 5, (Gill & McMillan; Dublin, 1970)

Costigan, Lucy & Cullen, Michael, *Strangest Genius, The Stained Glass of Harry Clarke* (The History Press Ireland; Dublin, 2010)

Craig, Maurice, *The Architecture of Ireland from the Earliest Times to 1880* (B.T. Batsford Ltd; London, 1983)

De Breffini, Brian & Mott, George, *The Churches & Abbeys of Ireland* (Hudson Ltd; London. 1976)

De Burca Rare Books, *The Harry Clarke Collection*, Summer 2010

Diestalkamp, Edward, *Building Techniques & Architecture*, Paper given at the Georgian Group Symposium, Published as Late Georgian Classicism, 1987

Donnelly, Michael, 'Glasgow's Glorious Glass', *History Today*, Vol. 40, No. 5, 1 May 1991

Douglas Hyde Gallery, *Harry Clarke Exhibition 1979, A Monologue & Catalogue*, published to coincide with the Exhibition (TCD; Dublin, 1979)

Dowling, William, 'Harry Clarke, Dublin Stained Glass Artist', *Dublin Historical Record*, 1960

F.S., 'Fr Mathew & Temperance', *The Capuchin Annual*, Dublin, 1930

Gordon Bowe, Nicola, *The Life & Work of Harry Clarke (1889-1931)*, Vol. 1-3, Thesis, TCD, 1981

Gordon Bowe, Nicola, *The Life & Work of Harry Clarke* (Irish Academic Press; Dublin, 1989 and History Press Ireland; Dublin, 2012)

Gordon Bowe, Nicola, Caron, David & Wynne, Michael, *Gazetteer of Irish Stained Glass* (Irish Academic Press; Dublin, 1989)

Gordon Bowe, Nicola, 'Symbolism in Turn of the Century Irish Art', *Irish Arts Review*, 1989/90

Gordon Bowe, Nicola, *The Stained Glass of Harry Clarke 1889-1931*, Catalogue to the Exhibition 2/5/1988-3/6/1988 (Fine Arts Society; London, 1988)

Gloag, John & Bridgewater, Derek, *A History of Cast Iron in Architecture* (George Allen & Unwin Ltd; London, 1943)

Grimes, Brendan, *The Architecture of Dublin's Neo-Classical Roman Catholic Temples, 1803-62*, Ph.D Thesis – Faculty of History of Art & Design & Complimentary Studies, NCAD, Dublin, 2005

Harrison, Martin, *Victorian Stained Glass* (Barne & Jenkins; London 1980)

Hurley, Roger, *Walk Through the South Parish* (Lee Press; Cork, 2010)

http:/buildingsofireland.ie/niah/search.jsp?type=record&county=CC&regno=2 29/10/2012

Hurley, Richard, *Irish Church Architecture in the Eve of Vatican 2* (Dominican Publications; Dublin, 2006)

Hurley, Richard & Lamour, Dr Paul (eds), *Sacred Places: The Story of Christian Architecture in Ireland* (RIAI & USUA; Dublin & Belfast, 2000)

Jefferies, Henry Alan, *Cork – Historical Perspective* (Four Courts Press; Dublin, 2004)

Keohane, Frank, *James & George Richard Pain – Architects of Cork's Golden Age* (Thesis, UCD, Department of Architecture, 2002)

Kerrigan, Colm, *Fr Matthew & The Irish Temperance Movement 1838-49* (Cork University; Press, Cork, 1992)

Larkin, Fr Pascal OFM Cap., 'The Capuchins in Cork', *The Capuchin Annual*, 1976

Lee, David, *James Pain – Architect* (Limerick Civic Trust; Limerick, 2005)

Lee, David, *Georgian Limerick 1714-1845, Vol. 1*, David Lee & Christine Gonzales (eds), (Limerick Civic Trust and FÁS; Limerick, 2000)

Lewis, Michael J., *The Gothic Revival* (Thames & Hudson; London, 2002)

Little, Joyce, *Stained Glass Marks & Monograms* (National Association of Decorators & Fine Art Society, London)

Lysaght, Marian, *Fr Matthew OFM Cap. – The Apostle of Temperance* (Four Courts Press; Dublin, 1983)

McCarthy, Kieran, *Cork Heritage* http://corkheritage.ie/?page_id=980 27 February 2013

McCarthy, Michael, *Studies in the History of Art* (Four Courts Press; Dublin, 2005)

McCarthy, Michael & O'Neill, Karina (eds), *Studies in the Gothic Revival* (Four Courts Press, Dublin, 2008)

McDermott, Matthew J., *Ireland's Architectural Heritage – An Outline History of Irish Architecture* (Folens & Co. Ltd; Dublin, 1975)

McNamara, T.F., *Portrait of Cork* (Watermans; Cork, 1981)

McParland, Edward, *Church or Chapel? The Case of St. Mary's Church, Pope's Quay, Cork*, Gillespie, Raymond & Foster, R.F., Editors, *Irish Provincial Cultures in the Long 18th Century – Making the Middle Sort, Essays for Toby Bernard* (Four Courts Press; Dublin, 2012)

Maguire, John Francis M.P., *Fr Matthew – A Biography*, Eason & Son, Dublin. Edited and Abridged by Rosa Mulholland – Centenary Year of Temperance Movement

Martin OSA, Fr F.X., *A Study of Francis Lavalin Nugent (1569-1655) Agent of the Counter Reformation* (Methuin & Co. Ltd; London, 1966)

National Inventory of Architectural Heritage – http://www.buildingsofireland.ie 04 February 2013

Neary, Revd Paul, OFM Cap., *Analystic Biographical History of Irish Province, c1919* (Irish Capuchin Provincial Archives, Dublin)

O'Dwyer, Frederick, *The Architecture of Deane & Woodward* (Cork University Press; Cork, 1997)

O'Mahoney, Fr Brendan, OFM Cap., *Fr Mathew, Social Reformer*, Paper given at International Temperance Conference (Commemoration of the 150th anniversary of Fr Mathew's death), Cork, October 2006

Parissien, Stephen, 'Ironwork – A Brief Guide to Georgian Ironwork', *The Georgian Group Guides*, No. 8, Kent, England

Quinn, P.F., *Fr Mathew's Crusade – Temperance in 19th Century Ireland & Irish America* (University of Mass; Press, Amhurst & Boston, 2002)

Rogan, Revd Patrick, *Fr Theobald Mathew – Apostle of Temperance* (The Catholic Book Club; London, 1945)

Rogers, Revd Patrick, *Fr Theobald Mathew – Apostle of Temperance* (Browne & Nolan Ltd; Dublin, 1943)

Ruskin, John, (Links, J.G. ed.), *The Stones of Venice* (De Capo Press; New York, 1960)

Rykwent, Joseph, *The First Moderns – The Architects of the 18th Century* (The MIT Press; USA, 1980)

Scareibman, Susan, *Introduction to the Capuchins* (The Thomas MacGreevy Archive, 1999) http://www.macgreevy.org/style=text&sources.com.cpa.xm/&action=show 10/11/2011

Scott-Richardson, Douglas, *Gothic Revival Architecture in Ireland* (Garland Publishing Inc.; New York & London, 1983)

Shaw, Fr Nessan OFM Cap., *The Irish Capuchins – Record of a Century, 1885-1989* (Capuchin Publications; Dublin, 1985)

Sheehy, Jeanne, *J.J. McCarthy & the Gothic Revival in Ireland* (Ulster Architectural Heritage Society; Belfast, 1977)

Sisk Book Committee & Project, *Building a Business – 100 Years of the Sisk Group* (Associated Editions, Dublin)

Snoddy, Theo, *Dictionary of Irish Artists – 20th Century* (Merlin Publishing; Dublin, 2006)

Stanislaus OSFC, Fr, *Historical Jottings Re The Church of the Most Holy Trinity*, (Fr Matthew Church) (Irish Capuchin Provincial Archives, Dublin)

Stephens Curl, James, *Georgian Architecture* (David & Charles; Newton Abbot, Devon, 1993)

Turpin, John, 'Reorganisation & Destruction of Irish Catholic Churches', *Studies*, 911;363, 2002.

Walsh, Revd J.J., *The Capuchins in Ireland* (Capuchin Annual; Dublin, 1952)

White, James & Wynne, Michael, *Irish Stained Glass – A Catalogue of Irish Stained Glass Windows by Irish Artists in the 20th Century* (Gill & McMillan in association with The Furrow; Dublin, 1963)

Williams, Jeremy, *A Companion Guide to Architecture in Ireland* (1837-1921) (Irish Academic Press; Dublin, 1994)

Windele, John & Coleman, James, *Historical & Descriptive Nature of the City of Cork From its Foundation to the Middle of the 19th Century*, (written 1837). Revised, abridged and annotated by James Coleman 1930 (Hon. Sec. Cork Historical & Archaeological Society) (Guy & Co. Ltd; Cork, 1930)

Wynne, Michael, *Irish Stained Glass* (Irish Heritage Series) (Eason & Sons Ltd; Dublin, 1977)

Sources

Abbey Stained Glass Co., Dublin.

Capuchin Annual

Cork Corporation

Cork Council of Trade Unions

Cork Examiner

Dublin City Libraries

Irish Architectural Archive, Dublin.

Irish Capuchin Provincial Archives, Dublin

Irish Penny Magazine

National Inventory of Architectural Heritage

National Irish Visual Arts Library (NIVAL), NCAD, Dublin

National Library of Ireland (NLI), Dublin

NLI Manuscript Library, Dublin

Trinity College Dublin (TCD) Manuscript Library

Index

Visit our websites and discover thousands of
other History Press books.

www.thehistorypress.ie
www.thehistorypress.co.uk

The History Press Ireland